NAMED AFTER LEGENDS

NAMED AFTER LEGENDS

SELF-DISCOVERY AMID THE SHADOWS OF GIANTS

STEVLAND MARTIN MALCOLM POLITE

atmosphere press

This book is dedicated to all my family and friends.
Without you, there's no me.

INTRODUCTION

My father named me after his heroes. Igniting a set of expectations based on what I can only assume was his vision of who he wanted me to be or be like. Cementing my identity with an inherent responsibility to honor these legends. However, I was born into a society that amplifies stereotypical versions of Black men, not Black heroes. Versions whose skin color served as the basis of their entire identity in the eyes of the world. Linked to negative character associations like thug, thief, or addict. And some of us are. A lot of us are victims too, though. Victims of a system designed to kill us. But that's why our heroes matter so much. Because the world we live in has consistently expressed the way it expects us to be. It continues to spew derogatory terms at us so that we eventually believe that's who we are. It's a strategy as old as time. Gaslighting at its finest. We get surrounded by images that portray the darkest sides of our humanity without shedding equal, let alone more, light on the fullness and value of our rich culture. One of the aims of the oppressors is to make sure the oppressed never gain the courage to escape the confines of their control. This courage begins with the belief that we can, in fact, take control of our own lives. Belief in our greatness comes from questioning everything. Because the truth will set us free. My journey to my truth started with a simple question: Who am I? If what I thought about myself was a lie, I knew it would be difficult to face my truth. And sometimes it was. But more and more, I started to become more grounded in my truth. So, I committed to continuing my self-education, not only about who I am but about who and what I could become.

Being named after Black legends comes with this daily reminder of the potential greatness we possess, how different we can be and, more importantly, how impactful our voice can be when we stand firm in our beliefs. But it did not offer much room for finding my own identity or for crafting my own belief system. A task that seemed impossible when I was growing up and when surviving my environment consumed most of my thoughts. What I did have, however, was this intense urgency to attain a better life. For the first eighteen years of my life, I felt trapped in a system of government control that was designed for me to fail, from public housing to the urban public school system of New York City. It wasn't until I went away to a private university that I recognized the disparities in living standards between my community and non-Black communities—and even other Black communities. The moment I recognized this, I decided I was going to use my time there for unprecedented exploration. I had never had so many opportunities presented to me. And I wanted to try them all. And I did, as much as was physically possible anyway, but now I can't help but ask myself: What does it all boil down to? How have these experiences shaped the man I am today? How can I stand firm in my beliefs like the legends I'm named after if after traveling the world trying to find myself, I still don't have a full grasp of who I am. There came a point when I had to understand that the answers I was looking for were inside of me. I just had to look. Exploring the world seemed easy compared to the work of exploring my inner self, which proved to be my greatest challenge. But it came with a reward unmatched by anything else I have experienced on this earth.

As a Black man in America, who is named after legends, I knew I had to approach my journey of self-identification like a legend. Which morphed into a journey of unprecedented exploration of self. I had never taken so much time to think about my mental and spiritual self. I found healing by breaking down stigmas, traumatic conditioning, and grief to find purpose in the form of a unique path that could lead me to become a legend in my own right.

For a large part of my life, my identity resided in my name. My dad, Richard Polite, named me Stevland Martin Malcolm Polite. After Stevie Wonder, Dr. Martin Luther King Jr., Malcolm X, and himself. I think it's fair to say he was proud to have a son and continue the Polite name. I imagine him pouring so many hopes and dreams into me with that name, knowing that our lineage, or at least what we can trace back to, is full of stories of survival and service just like the heroes he named me after.

My name always serves as a conversation starter. When I meet new people, I'm often confronted with a "Wow, are you a Polite person?" joke, as these new acquaintances amuse themselves with their perceived cleverness before realizing that I've probably heard that one before. And then there are those who let their bias convince them that my name must be pronounced with an accent. (No, it's not pronounced Po-LEET-ay.) Sharing the origins of my name is always fun, though. Most people I've come across don't know that Stevland is Stevie Wonder's birth name. So, they walk away from our encounter with a new fact, and I always feel good about sharing that experience with people, providing a little seed of knowledge that may stick with them forever. I love my name. However, there's an imposed veneration that comes with it. There's so much meaning and symbolism in the brevity of a name, and mine caused a lot of confusion for me regarding the symbolic power, if any, of my existence. Prompting questions like: Do I have any genius-level talents like Stevie? Do I believe in integration like Martin or separation like Malcolm? Do I become my father? Do I get to choose? And if so, how can I measure up to the bar that's been set?

My quest to answer these questions and untangle all the chords that had been plugged into me has been gut-wrenching. Matching in intensity with my journey to corporate, and entrepreneurship America. The odds against me are stacked all around. My approach thus far has been to throw my ideas in the air, see where they land, and if they are out of reach, pivot. Going after whatever was within arm's reach. Winging it as I steamrolled my way through every obstacle. Enduring all the punches of failure and highs of success along the way.

It's been the pressure of the expectations placed upon me and those I placed on myself mixed with the difficulties of life that have both propelled me and knocked me the fuck out; I'm talking TKO. But what I've learned over the years is that the only thing that separates a legend from everyone else is the conviction to never give up. It's how I was able to go from Lehman Village Housing Projects in East Harlem to stepping onto the world stage and educating myself at some of the best schools on the planet. Creating a rare foundation for a Black man that comes from where I'm from. A foundation that can't be taken away from me and will forever be etched in my legacy. A foundation that I hope the next Black boy from the projects can look to for a full view of what it takes to make it out, mistakes and all. I was able to build a foundation for success because I never gave up, especially in the face of adversity. Fueled by my curiosity about all the things society told me I couldn't be, do, or have.

It's been the clarity that came with coming out of the bubble of other people's expectations of me that's been the most liberating. I found freedom in myself. In this book, I detail what that process was like for me. It's an inward journey that reflects my upbringing as a Black man in America with a dream and a view, albeit obstructed. I spent two years on this journey and my hope is that my story can inspire Black men to take the time to look inward. It's been one of the most fulfilling journeys of my life and I can now, more proudly than ever, say I know who I am.

INTRODUCTION

There's often a story that we tell ourselves during certain stages of life. A story that's usually one-sided and shaped based on our very real perception of our personal experiences. But there's no such thing as a one-sided story and everyone's version holds weight in the uniqueness of its existence. Telling our stories is how we move the needle toward consensus, compromise, and the foundation of democracy. It's how we learn to live with each other on the one planet that we have and how we highlight the similarities of billions of individuals living the gift of the human experience. When we focus on our similarities, we move a little closer toward the eradication of hate for ourselves and others. During my healing journey, I found that my mind was typically biased toward certain views because of the stories I'd tell myself. It was much easier for me to believe what I'd been conditioned to believe, rather than put myself in someone else's shoes to understand their point of view. I believed my thoughts. Coming to grips with views other than my own meant stepping out of my comfort zone and widening my lens so I could get a full picture. Elevating my consciousness beyond the self-aggrandizing views that led to my survival.

Changing my perspective completely altered how I viewed myself, my experiences, and my relationships. I had to remove the lens of the victim and tell myself a different story. A pivotal step in my journey toward healing. I knew the only way I could thrive was to free my mind of the victim mentality that kept me operating in survival mode. When I put on the lens of responsibility, the stories that once played so vividly in my mind were all of a sudden muddled with uncertainty. This is why I forced myself into deep reflection as part of my commitment to healing myself.

The urge for me to begin my inner healing work stemmed from tragic losses I'd experienced. I needed to take control of my mental health after depression and anxiety tried to kill me. It prompted thoughts that had me questioning if I would be better off not being alive. The pain I experienced felt unbearable.

I didn't understand these stories that were playing in my head. There was this assertive voice I didn't recognize, and it was drowning out the voice I knew to be mine. This new voice was dangerous. It was loud and full of destructive thoughts. It was cancerous, and I had to figure out how to remove it to survive. I had a vision for my life and I knew I wouldn't be able to step into that vision and thrive if I couldn't find the voice that reflected the thirty-year-old man I'd fought so hard to become. I started my search by examining the stories I'd been telling myself about myself, then made my way to understanding my perception of the world around me.

"Every society has its protectors of the status quo and its fraternities of the indifferent who are notorious for sleeping through revolutions. But today our very survival depends on our ability to stay awake, to adjust to new ideas, to remain vigilant and to face the challenge of change."

- Dr. Martin Luther King Jr.

PART 1:

SURVIVE, BY ANY MEANS NECESSARY

LEHMAN VILLAGE

If I had to pinpoint a moment in time when I decided I wanted more out of life, I'd say it was when I was around thirteen years old. I found myself on a battlefield in the middle of a turf war I had nothing to do with. Met with the reality of violence as a survival tactic, at that moment, I chose not to engage. It's a weird feeling being in a brawl; there's a natural attraction to violence when you're willing to do whatever it takes to survive. And growing up in a housing project in East Harlem, in the '90s during the war on drugs, made me all too familiar with the rush of adrenaline that came with trying to survive. I've witnessed this rush triggering violent reactions to threats more times than I'd like to admit. I'd often find myself constantly moving in and out of this adrenaline rush, where I've resorted to doing whatever it took to survive, but I never resorted to violence. I was exposed to violence as a way of survival at a young age because it was the general mindset of the environment I was in, but it was never in my true nature. My adrenaline rush came from avoiding violence, surviving by escaping the madness instead of diving headfirst into it. I often thought that made me cowardly. But as I've gotten older, I realize that I was the one with the courage. I was my own leader, and the skills I'd developed would take me to heights higher than anyone I knew had been. Sometimes the need for violence in my neighborhood was momentary, and sometimes it was a lifestyle. Any perceived weakness could put you into the prey category for those who hunted for sport. People also felt the need to prove themselves in my neighborhood. And a lot of times that need was real, to showcase you're not one to be preyed upon. And sometimes, that need was mixed with ego and insecurities that made for deadly combinations. For me, though, I never felt the need to prove myself or follow the herd, and that made me an outcast. But it also made me deeply dependent on myself, building my confidence in my ability to survive in my own way.

The Lehman Village Housing Projects, where I grew up, weren't very different from other government-owned apartment complexes that were created for low-income families throughout the country. The buildings were typically dilapidated due to minimal maintenance. The tenants ranged from low-income families or anyone who'd been displaced due to circumstances out of their control, to hustlers, gang bangers, and others who glorified being hood rich and famous. But, for the most part, Black families often didn't have the wealth or access to capital to overcome their dire circumstances. My maternal grandparents, Gus and Gladys, lost their Harlem home in a fire and were forced to move into the Lehman Village Housing Project with their five kids. My grandfather was the sole income earner in their household, as my grandmother was a stay-at-home wife and mother. Government housing was often the most viable option for low- and one-income families in areas like New York City, where the high-cost housing market pushed private options out of reach. Black people were typically left out of benefiting from economic opportunities in both the private and public sectors, which is why Black people were the main benefactors of these government-owned housing projects.

Being surrounded by family and friends is what made the community aspect of living in government housing the most bearable, at least for me. Because the risk of getting stuck in an old, run-down, piss-filled elevator on a hot summer day was worth it once you reached your destination. My destination was always apartment 11C where family, friends, and loved ones congregated, often around food, for conversation and love. Despite the conflicts that were bound to happen given the lack of room to breathe when living in such close quarters, love and loyalty was that constant I knew I'd always be able to find. Community is where we, as a people, create culture that others so nonchalantly appropriate. But the price we had to pay for that culture was high and we sometimes had to pay with our lives. Because lack of resources made us resourceful, it also made for terrible physical and mental health conditions. Our creativity comes from needing to be resourceful in a world that continues to oppress us and pin our backs against walls. But we always find a way, and I believe that's the essence of our culture. Diamonds can't be formed without pressure though.

Despite the many wars I'd been forced to fight on my own fronts, the government continues to fight its war against me and other Black people by bringing the police to our front doors. The highly policed corners, corridors, hallways, parks, and ball courts within the small radius of our block in Lehman made it feel like we lived in an authoritative, tyrannical, police state under constant surveillance by racist white cops. It created this cyclical system of fathers and father figures being taken away from us, leaving our Black women and young Black children needing to do whatever it took to provide for themselves and survive. They forced us into close quarters, knowing that crime would be inevitable, because that's human nature, and they made sure they were there to catch any offenders. And when there were no crimes to catch, they knew enough about our movements to target us and completely fabricate charges and evidence against us. Making it painstakingly difficult for many, especially Black men, to escape the thralls of a system designed specifically for our demise. It happened to my little brother, Jordin, once. The cops stopped him and his friends and planted a knife on him, then arrested him, and brought him to the precinct for processing. I believe that was their goal. They wanted to make sure they had every young Black man in the system somehow. Because once you're in, they'll always have precedent to label you a criminal. Luckily for my brother, we had family in law enforcement. My parents marched to the precinct and demanded that they let my brother go and completely remove his name from the system.

The close proximity of rivals and government-sponsored oppressors always heightened the possibility of conflict. Within the small communities, there were only so many spots at the top, and everyone wanted them. The glamour of the "top" is what a lot of the youth aspired to. Whether it was by way of hustling, sports, or rap. I wasn't interested in any of those. Recruiters weren't coming to the hood to recruit sports and entertainment talent. If you didn't have a strong support system that advocated for you or helped you find the necessary opportunities, then that dream was out of the question. The dream was real though, and society perfected the sales pitch targeted at black youth. Don't get me wrong, there's plenty of talent in the hood. But even if you are as good as Jordan or as talented an MC as HOV, sometimes spending money on transportation to your future is out of the question. Especially if you have to choose between chasing a dream or feeding your family. For many of us, hustling was often the most feasible option to get money. It was for sure the most prevalent in the hood. Even if you were hustling just to provide for your family. But that's part of the trap. I've seen so many dreams die at the hands of this trap. My dreams became my most valuable asset. It's what I protect with my whole heart. The lifestyle of the trap meant that if wandering into someone else's proclaimed territory meant feeding your kids, even at the risk of inciting conflict, then so be it. And, at the same time, when your territory was being threatened, you'd do anything to keep it from falling.

This, in essence, is how I found myself at the edge of a park fence with a brick in my hand with intentions to defend myself and the four corners of my block. It was Lehman Village vs.

Carver, two housing projects that were directly across the street from each other. I didn't know anything about the events leading up to this brawl. It seemed like it came out of nowhere. This was a time when everyone was always outside. I remember suddenly everyone started running and yelling. It was during the day, so the sea of people all moving together was easy to spot. So, I started running too. Following the herd when someone yelled at me, "Come on, we're going to Carver." In my hood when you're called upon, you join the fight. It's part of the inherent loyalty that comes with being a part of the community. I didn't think twice about it. I just ran. When I got around the corner and saw the chaos that was ensuing, I picked up a brick off the sidewalk and was ready to charge. But, in a moment of clarity, I realized that picking up that brick meant using it. And I wasn't about to bash someone's skull in or risk having the same done to me for no reason. So, I decided to simply put the brick down, turn around, and walk away.

This was probably the first time in my adolescent life that I truly chose myself. At the time, I didn't realize the significance of that moment or how much it would dictate who I'd become. I definitely didn't see it as a courageous act; in fact, I thought it meant the opposite. But despite the pressure or potential backlash, I decided not to follow the herd. To forge my own path, even if it was a lonely one. Luckily, I always played the shadows. I never wanted to be a gangster or hood famous, so there were no expectations or incentives for me to prove that I was strong enough to fight. Which made my decision to walk away seemingly insignificant in the grand scheme of this battle. I often felt like the underdog growing up, in the shadows of my cousins Raylin and Coco big personalities. We were like the three amigos, and their subscription to the the life our enviornment forced upon us helped me fly under the radar. And for most of my childhood I appreciated that. My survival was dependent on it.

I never aspired to the same things as everyone else in my community. I didn't want the life I saw others so desperately try to attain. It always led to either death or imprisonment, and I wanted something different. I didn't know what it was, but I believe that decision to walk away was really a decision to walk toward a search for a better life. I wanted a life that would match the ambition that I had. Don't get me wrong, I wanted my own mountaintop like everyone else, but what I aspired to looked like a top floor in one of the skyscrapers I walked by in Times Square whenever we mobbed to the AMC on a Saturday night. We went to see a movie or to hang out, trying to pick up girls, competing to see who could get the most numbers on any given night. Either way, though, I always took the time to look up and take in the enormity of my surroundings outside the confines of Lehman Village. My head was always in the clouds. And, as I aged into my teen years, I slowly began to realize that education was the path that was going to get me to my mountaintop.

Not too long after my decision to walk away from that fight, I got my chance to get a taste of this dream. When I was fourteen, my mom found out about an opportunity for summer youth employment. It wasn't like the summer youth program I did the year earlier, which was fun and a mess at the same time. I worked in a daycare center in Jefferson projects, with Raylin and Coco. Why they let fifteen-year-olds anywhere near young kids is beyond me, but it was fun. I loved being able to work with my cousins. I can always remember this year because of the NYC blackout of '03. Raylin and I were walking back to Lehman from Jefferson, about ten blocks, when everything went out. I remember scrambling to get candles and food because no one knew how long it would last. We thought it would only be for a short period, but it didn't end. Everyone was outside and we just decided to make the best of it. The government must've fixed the infrastructure to withstand the heat waves we were experiencing, and still are, because from my memory there hasn't been a blackout that bad since.

The next year I found myself on the subway with my mom heading to Queens to apply for a summer youth employment opportunity she had heard about from a friend. I didn't know what to expect, but I was surprised when I was placed at Empire State Development Corporation. This corporate opportunity was a huge step up from the day care I worked at the prior year. And all it took was a little initiative and support from my mom. Their offices were in Grand Central in one of those skyscrapers I never thought I'd be in. But here I was, this fourteen-year-old kid from Harlem placed in this position of relative privilege. I would never forget my manager, a Black woman who always looked out for me and made me feel welcome. I don't remember the work I was doing, but I remember the lifestyle. It was a lifestyle that I wanted. At this point, my family had moved to the Bronx, so I would get up every morning, put on business casual clothes, and make my way from our Bronx apartment near Burnside Avenue to midtown with all the middle-upper-class professionals. I got a taste of independence in a way I never had before, and I decided this was the life I wanted for myself. I laugh today about how difficult the journey to get back there actually was. I had no clue about the challenges and obstacles that awaited me, but I never gave myself the option of giving up. So even when my body physically screamed give up, I could never choose that option. I didn't have a handbook, blueprint, or manual of any kind. No one in my family had chosen this path, so I gave myself the power of choosing to succeed the day I walked away from that brawl. I wasn't just walking away from a fight; I was walking away from a way of life and toward a life that would take me around the world and expose me to many different cultures and ways of life. I was ultimately crafting my own path filled with adventure and a quest for understanding humanity.

UPWARD BOUND

High school was a time when I began to really look at life with hope and possibilities and when I began to experience the complexities and dualities of the world I was living in. There was never a dull moment at MCSM (Manhattan Center for Science and Mathematics). Especially with my crew, the REC. Amanda, Edwin, Donnell, Brian, Jorden, and Gabriel. We were cool, smart, and fly. We moved with intention and love for one another. I'm forever grateful for our time together. We always pushed each other to be better. You had to be cool, smart, and fly to roll with us. But as far as educational experience, there wasn't anything that spectacular about how we were taught. But within those days and years of basic learning were moments and experiences that were extraordinary. Like having an out-of-body educational experience within a rather mundane one. That's what happened to me that summer I spent taking classes at Columbia University. An opportunity that presented itself as a product of a failure. In order to receive a high school diploma in New York, students are required to take a number of standardized tests called Regents. Because passing the class wasn't enough to prove our comprehension, we were forced to take exams not designed for our comprehension but for our ability to pass a standardized exam. I'd always done relatively well on these exams and had learned early on that it was equally about knowing how to pass these exams as it was about understanding the actual material. However, the chemistry Regents Exam was a different beast and it was the only one that I didn't pass. I'd done well in my chemistry class, but I couldn't learn how to pass the state Regents Exam the first time I took it. After failing, I had a choice. I could either go to summer school to study for the retake or apply to a program called Upward Bound, an in-residence program for high school students at Columbia University. Thankfully, I was fortunate enough to get in. So instead of enrolling in mandatory summer classes for chemistry at my high school, I was able to enroll in a chemistry class offered by Columbia University.

It was a crazy experience for me because I'd lived in Harlem all my life, and up until I was sixteen years old, I had never been on Columbia's campus, which was just a few blocks away. This

Ivy League school was right in my backyard. I didn't even understand what an Ivy League school was at the time, even while I was there that summer. I only knew that there was something majestic about the place. The grand cafeteria, the amazing classrooms that made you want to participate, and most importantly the impressively engaged people, together created an energy unlike anything I'd experienced before. I took several summer classes during the program, including one on the history of New York City. It was a thrilling experience. It was the first time I thoroughly enjoyed classroom learning. I ended up acing my chemistry class and received a science award at the end of the program for how well I'd done.

It was my first experience with different learning environments and how I could excel in one environment and fail in another. This made me believe that the New York Public School system is designed for students of color in urban communities to fail because the environment that they foster seems more like a prison than an institution for learning. Ever since that summer at Columbia University, I knew that I only wanted to be in environments that could bring out the excellence in me. I loved not only that feeling of excelling at something but being recognized for it as well. I started believing that I deserved better and, given the right opportunity, I could be good at anything I put my mind to. Because of how well I did and the praise I received from these extremely smart professors, I felt that I could one day go to college. And maybe I'd study chemistry. I had yet to be introduced to something I was truly passionate about or the idea that I could make a living from my passion. What I had been introduced to that summer though was work ethic. And my incredible capacity to do and be more.

As my ambitions started to take shape, there was a hustle behind them. A hustle that I attribute to my pursuit of safety as I grew up in a neighborhood that was often not safe. Where I'd witnessed so many terrible things happen to good people as soon as they let their guard down. I never let mine down. But at some point, I started to experience more good than I ever knew possible. After that summer at Columbia, the bar for my aspirations started rising. How could I not want more? Experiencing greatness and tasting it felt like a high. And with my addictive personality, I wanted to taste more. I wanted my safety to reside in that feeling. I started to focus more on school, aiming for high grades instead of just coasting by. When I was preparing for my SATs, I took a Princeton Review prep course. The first time I took the practice exam, I did terribly. At this point, I knew that I wouldn't re-create that feeling I had at Columbia if I didn't focus. And that's what I did for the duration of the course. I ended up doing really well on the last practice exam. And then I received an award from Princeton Review for the most improved score out of all New York City students. And part of the award was four tickets to see *The Lion King* on Broadway.

It was my first Broadway experience. Until that point, my experience in the world-famous theater district was relegated to the AMC or Regal movie theater in Times Square with friends, often hanging around trying to pick up girls. This time was different, though. It was a magical evening for my family and me. We went to dinner beforehand and the entire experience felt like a scene out of a movie. It was a night in a new, more luxurious bubble. For the first time, I started to see the value of education and where it could take me. I was also starting to realize that I might actually be really smart. Seeing tangible rewards for my hard work helped me gain the confidence I needed to be successful in my future endeavors. I gained a strong sense of belief in myself and my abilities.

The summer of '04, the summer I studied at Columbia University, the summer between my sophomore and junior year of high school, solidified so much for me. The most important was the realization of my ability to do whatever I set my mind to. I loved everything about my experience at Columbia, except for the many rules we had to abide by. They let us taste the freedom that came with campus living but put rules in place that a lot of us in the program weren't used to. We had a curfew and could only leave the campus and venture out for about an hour each night during designated times. Our weekends were our own, but I'd spent mine working part-time at a public pool on the Upper East Side of Manhattan, cleaning the grounds in and around the pool, manning the locker room during open hours, and any and everything in between. I headed to work right after class on those early Friday afternoons and worked the entire weekend to bring in any extra cash that I could. During the week, we were only allotted one hour of free time in the evenings when we could leave campus. We couldn't go far, though; our advisors would stand on every corner for ten blocks down Broadway in bright Columbia-blue T-shirts to make sure none of us ventured beyond the allowed perimeter. We had to don the infamous Columbia colors as well, lighting up Broadway in Columbia blue to make sure we'd be easy to spot.

That summer Akon's biggest hit, "Locked Up," became our anthem. We would blast this song in our dorm rooms as an expression of how we felt about all the rules we had to follow, especially when curfew called for lights out at 10:00 p.m.

NATURALLY HUMAN

Fast forward six years after that summer at Columbia to fall 2010, I'm in Morocco camping overnight in the Sahara Desert during my fall break from my studies at the American University of Rome, and Akon's hit, "Locked Up," comes blaring from the flip phone of our Berber nomad guide. After spending a few days in the city of Marrakech, my friends and I decided to go on the camel trek into the Sahara before heading to the city of Fez. We drove ten hours into the desert in a tiny van that whipped through the narrow, winding, and pulchritudinous rolling hills of the colorful Moroccan countryside. We occasionally stopped to bask in the motherland's picturesque views and petrichor that engulfed us every time we stepped off the tiny van. The stops also served as a time for us to stretch our legs. It was a long, hot, arduous ride in the middle of nowhere. But I found myself content staring out the window of the van at the deep sea of rich red, orange, brown, and green earth.

When we finally arrived at our destination, at the edge of the Sahara Desert, we were directed to choose a camel for the last part of the trek, which we would ride for an additional two hours deeper into the desert. I hated that camel ride so much. It hurt like hell in my groin area, forcing me to cringe in anticipation every time we came across a new sand dune that caused the camel to suddenly drop and adjust accordingly. When it was time to ride back the next day, I begged our guide to let me walk alongside them but, unfortunately, I had to bear the pain for another two-hour trek back to the road for our ten-hour drive back to Marrakech.

That evening, after the initial camel trek, we arrived at a campsite that was already set up. We became quick friends with our guides after a day of activities, including dinner and a group firepit where we exchanged stories and talents with other travelers. I was fascinated by the nomadic lifestyle and couldn't pass up a chance to learn more about their way of life. Up until that point, the only thing I knew about nomads was the glorified versions of a pre-civilization way of life of explorers that I'd read about as a boy in history textbooks and not a modern alternative way of life that is still practiced. I could never have imagined I'd cross paths with some. I was kind of shocked to see that nomads roaming the earth, evolved yet devoid of societal norms and beliefs, still existed. I immediately tapped into the feeling of freedom I'd connected to. I knew I was a wanderer at heart and I rejoiced in knowing that impermanence was an option.

A few of the Berber guides, whom my friends and I had gotten close to, took us off the campsite that evening while everyone else was tucked away in their tents. We sat on top of a sand dune talking about life and watching shooting stars race across the pitch-black night sky. I'd never seen that many stars in my life, let alone shooting stars. We'd counted them as they flew by, making a wish every time. We saw what seemed like hundreds of shooting stars that night. All I know is that I've never experienced a night like it since. We talked about everything from relationships to politics and daily life. It was surprising how much we had in common despite the many differences in our lifestyles. Even our struggles seemed to be rooted in similar human elements. Like wanting to indulge in a vice but fearing persecution. I witness a car quickly pull up to our camp site to bring wine, which was illegal to drink. And it reminded me of the stealth mode I'd seen back home from friends and family wanting to indulge in marijuana. This was the point during the night when one of the guides pulled out the mobile flip phone, which had probably been discontinued for years in the US, and started to play music from it. He said he loved hip-hop and started to play his new favorite song. "Locked Up" by Akon.

I was immediately transported to that dorm room at Columbia six years earlier. I was in the middle of an African desert, thinking about my hometown and how much of an impact it had on my life. And it was at that moment that I not only realized the power of music to transcend time and geography but the power of humanity to unite under common feelings and emotions no matter our culture, our land, or our skin color. For us in that moment, it was the feeling of yearning for freedom from our current realities that united us.

UNFORGIVABLE

The pressure of excelling often carries a heavy burden for others like me who also have to deal with the pressure of staying alive. I'd grown up around a lot of death and sorrow. I'd experienced it often growing up in East Harlem. I've had to attend countless funerals for people of all ages. One that often weighs heavily on me happened when I was about twelve or thirteen. A little girl was shot by a stray bullet that was intended for someone else. She was in the wrong place at the wrong time. I didn't know the girl well, but I knew her brother and the shooter. The trauma of witnessing the destruction of the lives of so many people at once is surreal. There's no way to truly understand the enormity of it all, especially at such a young age. Growing up in that environment really normalized the death and destruction of people that looked like me. I had become desensitized to death at an early age. I've seen crackheads here today, roaming the streets looking for their next fix, then gone the next day. I've had neighbors who never made it home, etc. Death was very much a part of life and I'd grown to keep the grief that came with it at arm's length.

There was a point where I felt my family was immune to it. That I was immune to death getting too close to me. I thought my efforts to steer clear of death had been enough. It was definitely naivete on my part. I was a young dreamer, so terrified of death and what it meant that I just chose to believe it couldn't reach me. But soon enough, it started getting closer.

After the summer at Columbia, I felt comfortable working during the school year. So, my junior year, I got a job at Jamba Juice, where I worked for a year and a half, up until I went away to college. To this day, it's been one of the best jobs I've ever had. I looked forward to going to work. We had so much fun. I don't know if it was youthful ignorance, but I've been chasing that feeling of how work is supposed to feel and the joy of building real relationships and believing in the mission. I also worked with my best friend Amanda so that could've had a large part in how I felt about the job.

I built great relationships with many of my coworkers like my assistant manager, Steve. We both lived in the Bronx at the time, so we always rode the train together after we'd closed the store, which was in downtown Manhattan in the Chelsea area.

My mom sometimes picked us up and drove us home after our shift as it would be after midnight, and I had class in the morning. But, on the days we trekked it on the subway all the way uptown, we began to build a real friendship. We'd talk about everything on our hour journey through the boroughs. One day, he told me that he was gay, and that's been one of the most honest conversations I'd have with anyone to this day. I thought that it was extremely brave of him to open up to me about it, not knowing how I'd react, but it was a great lesson for me in how someone can own their truth. I didn't know anything about his lifestyle, but I knew automatically that it wouldn't change anything about our friendship. It brought us closer as friends and forced me to challenge my perception of what gay men looked like and how they acted, as well as the false narrative that proximity and visibility can somehow make another person gay. During one of our conversations, he told me about his time after high school when he went off to college. To a "wannabe Ivy League," as he put it, a school in Philadelphia called Drexel University. He was an aspiring scientist but unfortunately had to drop out because of financial issues, which was typical for students of color at Drexel.

One day he got fired from Jamba Juice for reasons unknown to me. But I believe it was because of his unorthodox management style. Steve never took himself too seriously and found a way to strike a balance of respect and friendship with his employees. After he left, we stayed in contact, but our conversations slowly decreased over time. A few months later, I was doing a run to another store on Eighth Avenue to pick up some supplies with one of my leads who was on duty that day. As we were walking back, she told me that Steve passed away. She detailed how he got meningitis, which quickly led to complications with his brain. I don't remember the details besides the fact that it spread quickly, killing him within a matter of weeks. This was the first time I'd experienced someone young, in their twenties and seemingly healthy, die from health complications as opposed to murder. I also found out that day that there are many forms of violence.

The family called the store to let us know the funeral details, but our general manager decided not to tell us and we missed his service. To this day, I don't understand why anyone would do that. I felt violated in a way that's difficult to explain. I felt the weight of anger and sadness equally, but knew I had to choose which one to give into, especially because I was still on the clock while all of this was being told to me. I decided to let go of the anger as it did nothing to honor my friend, but the sadness remained. I think it was the first time my heart broke. I had experienced death, disappointment, betrayal, and fear before, but never like this. Letting go of the anger left me with a grudge, one that I still struggle to forgive to this day. There's not much that a person could do to me that is unforgivable, but my general manager's actions was one of them.

A few weeks later, I was working at Jamba Juice behind the register when I got a call from my mom letting me know that a package had arrived from Drexel University. I quickly left my post and told her to open it and let me know what it said. She read that first line, letting me know that I had been accepted, and it was one of the happiest moments in my life. But standing there in that store, knowing Steve was no longer with us, made it bittersweet. But at least I had a chance to finish what he started at Drexel University.

I AM MY MOTHER'S SON

My mom had me when she was twenty-two, my dad was twenty-six. It wasn't until later in my life that I realized how difficult being such young parents must have been for them. They'd been together for a couple of years before having me. My mother was a special education teacher, and my father was a cab driver, local DJ, and rapper. They met at a party in Harlem.

My father and his best friend, Tracy, my cousin Raylin's father, drove up to Harlem from Queens at the request of my mom's cousin. They struck gold when they met my mom and my Aunt Denise, aka Niecy. Not knowing at the time that they'd be spending the next three decades together. The Thompson sisters were and still are a force to be reckoned with. Including my Aunt Shirell, aka BooBoo, the youngest of the three. They were all instrumental in helping me become the man I am today.

At the time I was born, I think it's fair to say that my parents were struggling in many ways. My mom had a very tough pregnancy, with me being born prematurely via an emergency C-section. She never let all the adversity stop her from being intentional in raising me though while making some hard choices along the way. My mom always tells us the story of how even after I was born, her mom wouldn't allow her and my dad to sleep in the same room together whenever he slept over. My grandmother was very strict in that regard, although clearly it didn't help, because rebellion is probably why I'm here today. So, my dad, on his cab salary, rented a rundown apartment in Queens that sat atop a now dilapidated store. I know this because he points it out to us any time we drive by it when we're in Queens. It always serves as a testament to how far they've come, but, it took a lot of hard decisions and sacrifices. My brother, Jordin, was born four years after me, and my mom decided it would be in her best interest to work for the city. She took the corrections officer exam, passed it, and spent fourteen years working in Rikers Island, the toughest jail in the country. She worked in the men's jail, surrounded by some of the worst criminals in the world, all to provide a better life for us. My father would later join her after a few stints at some other career opportunities, eventually rising in rank from officer to captain and then to assistant deputy warden.

Although my mom had to be tough at work, she was never too tough on us. She did her best to offer a balance to make sure we never ended up in the prison system. My father was very strict with me, though. I think it would've broken them to come to work and see us in jail. It would've broken us too; that was one of the reasons they worked so hard to make sure we had everything we wanted and more. My parents taught me a lot of great lessons growing up. "Let It Go," or "LIG it," is a phrase that my mom would always say to us that stuck with me. It's helped to shape how I move in this world. It's how I developed my ability to compartmentalize and not let the stressors of my environment affect my priorities. Instead of dwelling on issues, I learned to let them go and move on. This skill set the tone for me in how I would approach my studies in college. Taking on as much as I could because I was able to deftly switch between many different subjects. It's how I've come to define myself as a generalist. Someone who knows a little bit about a lot of things. But I can see now how this approach hasn't taught me how to go all in on one thing. But to be honest, I don't want to. I think it's a trap. But I've come to understand how I've used my approach to learning in the same way as my approach to relationships. Maintaining a generalist relationship with myself and others.

Over time, I developed this ability to be OK with letting things go, to move on, to push a subject to the back of my mind and bring forward the next thing I need to work on. As a Black man in America, this skill gave me an advantage in surviving in a place where most people that look like me don't, in a society where we're being attacked on all fronts. The tolerance that I've built to those attacks is in direct relation to my ability to compartmentalize. Because if I didn't, I knew I would've been too overwhelmed to achieve all the things I wanted. Because if I let every instance of negative news like someone I know getting arrested or shot or another police shooting of an unarmed Black man or every time I experience racism consume my thoughts, there'd be no room left for me.

Another lesson my mom taught me was the inevitability of becoming whole again after any kind of disruption. When I was young, I'd go to the Central Park public pool with my brother, cousins, and friends. It was a short walk from my grandfather's apartment, and we'd hike through the parks finding shortcuts through off-the-beaten paths until we reached the entrance, or we bypassed the entrance altogether if the line was too long. One summer day, we closed the park out after a fun-filled day and were ready to head home when I realized that someone had broken into my locker and stolen everything I had, including my clothes and sneakers. Here I was wet with no shoes or dry clothes in sight. I was able to call my mom, so she could bring me a change of clothes and sneakers to walk home in (this was back when we actually had to memorize phone numbers). After what seemed like a grueling wait, she not only showed up with everything I needed but she had a fresh pair of all-white Air Jordan 9s. She didn't just make me whole again, she made me better. At that moment, she showed me that a setback is just setting me up for an even greater comeback. From the moment she showed up to rescue me, I'd forgotten all about what was taken from me.

My mom also taught me how to advocate for myself to get the best out of life. It's how I ended up going to a great middle school. A pivotal event that I can say with certainty, positively altered the direction of my life. Before I was set to graduate from elementary school, my parents moved us out of Harlem to the Bronx. I remember they took over the lease from my mom's longtime friend who was moving down south. That move, unknowingly to them, caused an issue when it came time for me to go to middle school. At the time, the rules of the New York Board of Education stated that public school students had to go to their zone school, meaning they had to go to the school that was closest to their home address. The school that was near our new address was not good as it was dangerous, had the worst teachers, and did not foster a good environment for learning. My mom did not accept them telling me that I had to go there. I'd been in Gifted and Talented (GAT) classes throughout my elementary school years, and she knew I would not be able to live up to my full potential if I went there. So, she took off work and went downtown to the Board of Education to lobby them on my behalf, with my grades in tow. Even when they told her no, she didn't give up. She kept going back, eventually convincing administrators to let me take a test to get into a better school in Manhattan. They were impressed by my mom as they claimed they'd never seen anyone advocate for their child the way she did. I passed the exam, went on an interview, and got admitted into Isaac Newton Junior High School for seventh and eighth grade. That was truly a defining moment for me that changed the trajectory of my education. I was able to witness my mom challenge the system and not just accept the status quo.

My mom was never the disciplinarian in our household; that was always my dad's role. My mom was the one who comforted me, spoiled me, and made sure I was always OK. She would stand in line at Foot Locker on Saturday mornings to make sure I got the new Jordans or leave the money on my dresser for me if she had to work. If you lived in Harlem then, you'd know that we didn't play about our sneakers and clothes. She made sure I was always on trend with whatever I wanted. She knew the importance of this for a young kid's survival, having grown up in Harlem herself, whether it was a pair of Prada sneakers or an expensive, oversized Marmot, the staple winter coat that anyone who was anyone donned in the early 2000s. She never questioned the ridiculousness of a trend, well, maybe once or twice. She and my dad just made sure I didn't have to do anything illegal to get it. I never needed anything from anyone or wanted what someone else had because my parents made sure I was always good. But there was one time in my life when my mom had to discipline me. And once was enough; I'd never forget it.

I was young, probably no older than ten years old when I got caught smoking a cigarette with a neighbor's daughter. We got caught by Raylin and Coco's godmother, Maylene, a longtime family friend, who was watching us at the time. We snuck into a room, went to the window, and lit the cigarette the way we'd seen others do a million times. When we got caught, the family friend told us she would tell our parents, but when my parents came home, they didn't say anything to me. The next morning, my mom made breakfast and we sat at the table, eating as a family. I'm not sure if my father was home or at work but I remember being more nervous than I'd ever been but also thinking that maybe she didn't know. It was an intense energy that still exists in me. Did she decide to not rat us out? I wish. As soon as breakfast was over, my mom called me into the bedroom, closing the door behind her as we entered. At that point, I was in the matrix. As she took her belt off, she proclaimed, with a stern yet calm voice. "So, you want to smoke cigarettes?" I knew at that moment I had fucked up, realizing that breakfast was my last supper. She was about to kill me. It was the first and only time my mother ever beat me. And I still vividly remember it two decades later. To this day, I've never had another cigarette.

Being a minority in most of the spaces I'm in, I also realized that not everyone can come with you on your journey. In fact, they're not supposed to. I've met a lot of people along the way, people who have helped me in some form or fashion during the different stages of my life. And while I feel grateful, I could never allow my attachment to someone or something hinder my growth or keep me stagnant. I've been groomed to let it go and move forward. If you're weighing me down, I have to let you go, no matter who you are. I worked too hard to become nimble and light enough to move in and out of any space I need to be in; it's probably why I have issues with commitment. But surrounding myself with people who are on a similar journey, moving in a similar direction and at a similar pace, with a similar mindset is key to me. I commit to that all day, every day. I knew they were out there. Finding them was the hard part, keeping them around was even harder, especially when your respective journeys start to head in different directions. Those are the hardest relationships for me to let go of, even when I know it's a necessity. It's very rare to find someone who impresses me. So, if you manage to, I know that you're someone I want to keep in my life. I'm aware that this path is a lonely one, but what's the alternative? Normalcy? I believe a lot of people are OK with normal, but that's not me. I already lived through hell, I want heaven here on earth for me and my family.

IN THE GAME

When I arrived at Drexel the first day as a starry-eyed freshman ready to take on the world, I wasted no time living the college experience and went to a party with my friend Ama, who I met in my dorm that first day. She was a freshman as well and her older brother, who was a junior or senior at Drexel at the time, invited her to a party at his fraternity house and she invited me to tag along. I met a guy there who was a chemical engineering major. He told me how much he didn't like his major and how limited the job prospects were. We talked for a while, and I was convinced that it wasn't for me. It didn't take much for me to change my mind. Having that insight helped solidify my decision. I knew it wasn't what I wanted to pursue. I had put myself in a position to network and learn and it began that first night, at a party. Before that night I didn't know what a professional career in the chemistry field would look like. I just knew that working in chemistry sounded good and I'd done so well in my chemistry class that summer at Columbia.

From that first night on, I knew I wanted to soak up as much knowledge as I could from as many people as possible to help construct the life that was best for me. I created a habitual approach of figuring out what wasn't for me to find my path through the process of elimination. That first night was a great lesson for me in the power of showing up. Because survival is in part putting yourself in positions with no clear immediate benefit other than access to a network of people. Relationships with others could end up having a crucial impact on your life. Sometimes we have no clue how things will turn out. But by keeping an abunbdant mindset opportunities started to just flow in for me.

I originally applied to Drexel as an accounting major, not knowing what an accountant did. After getting accepted, my plan was to change majors to chemical engineering. All I knew was that the application fee was free. I didn't think I'd get in until I went to a college fair at my high school. I visited their booth and talked with their representatives and their co-op opportunity stood out to me and the rep encouraged me to apply. I was sold by the idea that I could be working at a top firm in as early as two years. Making money was my main goal. I wanted to make sure I never had to live in a housing project again. I wish I had applied to more prestigious schools though.

I'm a naturally confident person, but I sometimes struggled with my own sense of self-worth. Growing my self-esteem was one of the reasons, even though my dad wanted me to go to Morehouse, a Historically Black College and University (HBCU), I chose a predominately white institution (PWI). As much as I love being Black, in my mind it would have been hard for me to stand out as an individual. At the time, all I wanted was the opportunity to be seen. And the PWI gave me a scholarship when the HBCU didn't offer any assistance at all. The money definitely made me feel seen and valued. My Black experience up until that point was great, but there was a part of the culture I didn't relate to. I wanted to expand my perspective to see what the world had to offer outside of my culture. Especially if I was going to try and change it. For the most part, I wanted to be in an environment that would maximize my ability to thrive regardless of racial demographics or cost. To be honest though, the application fee being free was probably the biggest reason I applied. I realize now how much an inclusive effort that is. I couldn't afford a bunch of $250 application fees. My school provided me a few waivers, but at the end of the day that application fee is a huge barrier for a lot of kids wanting to apply to college. With the common app, I ended up applying to a total of eighteen schools and got into 17. If I'd known then what I know now, I would have tried my luck at the top 18.

When it was time for me to decide which college to attend, I visited a bunch of the schools I got into so I could determine the best fit for me. When I visited Drexel, I knew immediately it was the place for me. The energy there was unmatched, and it did not disappoint. Its slogan, "Ambition Can't Wait," sums it up. My ambition could no longer wait. I had to get it all out and Drexel seemed like the best place to help me do that. Despite all the struggles that came with it, it ended up being the best decision for me; I did what I set out to do. It was a new experience for me, one that I relish and one that prepared me for the real world, with all its possibilities and disappointments, as much as it could.

When I entered Drexel, I thought I would study chemistry, but it wasn't backed by anything substantial. Only from an experience I had. It wasn't something I was passionate about and I had no clue how that would translate into making money. But the more I learned about all the different possibilities, the more evolved my goals and aspirations became. All I knew was that I wanted to be a part of something bigger than myself. This search turned into a never-ending rat race. I entered a new world that I'd have to continuously try to fit into and prove myself; the spotlight was always on. Every time I walked into a classroom and I was the only person of color, it always seemed like a spotlight automatically turned on and shined its light right on me. I didn't need to see the stares; I could feel the eyes on me from students and professors. There was no such thing as blending in. I never questioned if I should be there though. I know a lot of people who questioned their belonging, developing imposter syndrome, but I never felt that at Drexel. It would definitely come later though. On day one, I recognized that I was just as good and deserving as every other student. Because of my background, I knew I had a gap in knowledge, and I'd have to catch up to some of the other students who had been top of their high school classes and in programs like Future Business Leaders of America. I never let that intimidate me. It was the challenge I wanted, so I just committed myself to working harder than everyone else. That was my way of leveling the playing field. To be honest, it was a lot of work, but it wasn't that difficult. I had a knack for knowing what to focus on and when so that I could optimize my time.

That was my edge. My hustle mentality, born in Harlem, raised in pursuit of being someone greater, my ability to do more than most without breaking a sweat. It's how I graduated from Drexel's Lebow College of Business on time with 227 credits, 77 credits above the 150 required, despite a pletheora of hardships. With three majors in Finance, Marketing, and International Business and a minor in International Area Studies. It's how I learned a new foreign language and studied abroad twice at a time when studying abroad was rare. It's how I managed to become president of the Drexel Minority Achievement Program (DMAP) while working multiple jobs at a time, sometimes having three at once. I'm pretty sure I never actually slept in college. I was too busy winning national marketing competitions, getting flown out to Detroit to the General Motors headquarters to present to Chevrolet marketing and advertising executives, helping to lead the charge for hybrid and clean energy vehicles. I launched marketing campaigns for the navy to increase recruitment in Philadelphia; produced fashion shows with local vendors and live entertainment and produced award banquets for DMAP, whose mission focused on minority retention, honoring my peers; and attended award banquets where I was honored for my leadership and service to the Drexel and Philadelphia communities, something that was extremely important to me. Both communities helped students of color excel and mitigate risks that increased their dropout rate, and I was smart enough to utilize that community to do the same for myself. This was all while also trying to establish and maintain a modicum of a social life with my tribe. I don't know how I found the time, but

I partied a lot. I lived by the motto work hard, play hard. Any other free time was reserved for studying, typically throughout the night, while other people slept. As I reflect I realize that in my own way, taking advantage of all that was available to me was my own form of activism. A big Fuck You to the oppressors, like the police that hunted Black men in my neighborhood and Black neighborhoods across the country.

I became a member of DMAP before I even started at Drexel. I actively searched for minority student organizations on Facebook during the summer before my freshman year. I reached out to the President at the time and he let me know that they were looking for a freshman recruiter to join the executive board. I didn't hesitate to put my name in the ring for it. I loved the mission of the organization and I was actively involved in making sure the freshman felt welcome while helping to plan various events throughout the year.

I found that I was a natural leader and by my second year I decided to run for President of the organization. It ended up being a tie between me and another more senior member of the board. And then the following year I became the sole president. It was a lot to juggle given my course load and all the other things that I was doing but I took my role very serious. It was a great learning experience for me. I made some mistakes, but we were able to accomplish some great things. Both my mistakes and accomplishments as a leader helped shape the leader I am today. I'm extremely grateful for that experience and to have had an amazing cohort of students who helped bring our ideas to fruition. I feel most proud about being able to host awards ceremonies to acknowledge and celebrate some of the excellence within our community. I learned that it's important to valid each other when we're in majority white spaces. And we don't have to wait for those leaders to do so. Wherever we are. We are enough.

During my time in the navy recruitment project, I was chosen as the head of Research and Presentation. It was a specialized class for select individuals charged with creating a marketing event at the Community College of Philadelphia (CCP) to increase enrollment on its campus. The entire team worked extremely hard on this campaign. It was my job to research and analyze perception and willingness to sign up for the navy before and after our campaign and document all our efforts that led up to a navy takeover day at CCP. When it was all said and done, it was my job to create a presentation to present our results to the navy. I locked myself in my room and spent ten straight hours compiling information from all the different teams and summarizing the results from mine, giving it my all as I knew it was a representation of the entire class. I spent a few hours making sure I had a compelling presentation with consistent formatting throughout. After our presentation, we received great feedback, but all I could focus on was my professor giving her critique in front of everyone. She said that she noticed some inconsistent formatting in the presentation. It was hard to hear being the only Black person in the class. The entire class was being judged on my work output. I wanted it to be perfect; I thought it was. I knew then I would have to work harder to prove myself. When I think of being Drexel Made, I think of a pursuit of excellence. I didn't look at it as being harder on me because I was a Black man. It fueled my ambition because here I was doing this work for the navy as a freshman. That one comment got me thinking about how to redeem myself. I wanted more experiences like this and I wanted to excel. It was a full circle moment for me too as my Dad is a navy veteran. It's where he started his career.

The navy project was part of my course load and at the time was an experience fairly new to Drexel. After the presentation, I immediately went back to my dorm room and looked up opportunities similar to it. I found a national marketing competition sponsored by Chevrolet. The competition was opened to all universities and called for a creation of a campaign for their new green car rollout. It was 2007, and the world was beginning to make clean energy vehicles more mainstream. I knew this would be a great chance to be at the forefront of this green movement. So, I commissioned my roommate, Shawn, and two other classmates that lived on my floor, Abby and Liz. I then convinced my business professor to sponsor us, as it was a requirement to enter the competition. After weeks of hard work, we came up with our campaign titled, "An American Green Revolution." It included a complete rollout of press releases, merchandise, tours, commercial scripts, target market analysis, and ready-to-go advertisements. We created ilookgoodingreen.com as a site to direct consumers to Chevrolet's website. It was impressive, if I do say so myself, so impressive that we beat out hundreds of teams across the country to be chosen as one of the top five teams to present to Chevrolet executives. We were the only undergraduate team chosen, a team of freshmen competing with four other teams from top MBA programs, chosen to figure out how to introduce a new energy concept to one of the biggest markets in America.

Chevrolet flew us to Detroit for our presentation, which would take place at the GM headquarters. It was the first time something like that ever happened to me. I wasn't used to catching flights yet. As we began to descend into the city, I looked out my window to see the all-black GM towers towering over the city as a symbol of its monolithic presence as a goliath and force to be reckoned with. I was headed directly into the action because of my ideas. I catapulted myself into the inner workings of a Fortune 500 company, going from the trenches of East Harlem to iconic boardrooms in a matter of months. At the time, I was nineteen and at the tail end of my freshman year of college. Things were happening really fast, and I knew I didn't want that feeling to end. The adrenaline rush of creating something for national reach within a short time frame was like no other. From that moment, the chase for more had begun and there was no way I was going back. The feeling of being treated like an executive was one I knew I wanted to recreate. With all the perks that came with it. The nice hotels, fancy restaurants, and getting my ideas out. We didn't win the competition, but I learned some valuable lessons that would stay with me forever; namely, that my ideas can open up whole new worlds for me. And more importantly they can really impact how we, as humans, live in this world. But whatever vision I have for the world, I know that I'll have to lead the charge to make it a reality, and this competition proved to me that I could.

THE COOLEST GUY IN THE WORLD

Being the first in my family to go to college, part of my motivation for working so hard and not taking no for an answer had come from wanting my grandfather, Gus Thompson, to see me walk across the stage. I never thought about going to college, it was never something that was discussed as an option, but his love was the glue that kept my family together in a way that paved the way for me. And in my mind, being the first to graduate from a 4-year university was my contribution to his legacy. I wanted him to see this tangible result of his commitment and sacrifice. That dream was shattered when my phone kept ringing while I was in an economics class at Drexel.

I kept sending the calls to voicemail because it could wait, I thought, and this class was tough enough. I was still early in my undergrad career, only my second year. The professor recognized my skill in economics and was attempting to get me to switch my major to economics, and I was thinking about it. But the calls didn't stop. I excused myself from class and went to call my dad back. When he told me that my grandfather was gone, I lost it and broke down right in the middle of the hall where my class was taking place. I got myself together and went back inside to let the professor know that I'd be leaving and would not be coming back for a while. I didn't do as well in that class as I should have, putting an end to any idea of switching to economics. I ruined my GPA and any chance I had of getting into the advanced statistics classes, derailing my plans for a future in quantitative finance.

Gus was the epitome of a great Black man. He was one of the coolest dudes you'd ever meet. Anyone who's ever had the pleasure of meeting him would agree with me. He was genuine. I get my cool and my cooking skills from him. He was a chef and nutritionist at a hospital before retiring and becoming the neighborhood's Barbecue King. While at Drexel, I always tried to fit time into my busy schedule for family and friends in New York. The weekend before my grandfather passed, I was in New York and had put time into my schedule to visit my him, but something came up and I never got the chance. I told myself that I'd come back the next weekend. New York is only a two-hour bus ride from Philly, so it was easy for me to commute. Unfortunately, that chance never came and the guilt of not making him a priority at that moment stayed with me for a long time.

All my grandparents are gone now. My grandparents on my dad's side were the most recent deaths of the four of them. We knew their deaths were coming and had our chance to say goodbye, which I'm thankful for. It helped a lot. I'd never had the opportunity to say goodbye before. My grandfather Rudolph Polite was a World War II vet and his homegoing, although sad, was honorable. My grandmother Beatrice died of colon cancer, and we were with her to the end. On my mom's side, my grandmother Gladys passed from diabetes when I was in middle childhood. I still vividly remember being told she was no longer with us. Her death is one of my earliest memory. I remember being upset that my cousins and I had to go to the neighbor's house while the adults took care of everything. I wanted to be with my family and was annoyed at the elderly lady who kept talking about my grandmother as if they were best friends. Although I was too young to fully understand everything that was happening, I was old enough to know that I wanted to do something to help in some way. But I couldn't. That tension and helpless feeling are what I remember the most. But I saw how strong my grandfather was. He was a model for us on how to live life and handle death. And so after his death, I forged on. I knew it's what he would have wanted. Back to school I went.

BUBBLE LIFE

My decision to stay in business was one of the greatest decisions I could've made. I experienced poverty but found myself with opportunities to witness wealth. Although I didn't fully understand what capitalism was, I felt the power of money. And then I became infatuated with the world after my first international trip during my first spring break in March 2007. My roommate, Shawn, who was from California, found a flight to London for $400. I immediately thought to myself, Wow that's within reach. To fly halfway around the world for $400 seemed like a miracle, even if I didn't have the $400 to go. I didn't even have a passport, but Shawn seemed to have some experience with travel. I had been on a plane a couple of times before, one time flying to Florida to Disney World with my family, but didn't know much about fyling or the associated costs. But Shawn reassured me that it was a good opportunity, and I should try to join. I was only a quick two-hour drive away from home and never even thought about being that far away without my family with me. I thought about how my roommate couldn't see his family as frequently as I did, yet he was still using his break to travel abroad instead of going home. I was intrigued. There had to be something great about traveling and I wanted in.

After finding out about the trip to London, I went home to our Bronx apartment, where I lived with my parents and little brother for years before going away to school. While on my way home, I prepared a speech to try and convince my parents to buy the plane ticket for me. Less than a year in business school and I was already learning how to create presentations to convince others to buy into whatever I was selling. I presented the trip as a once-in-a-lifetime experience, laying out all the details and adding that it could be an early birthday present. Little did I know there'd be a lot more once-in-a-lifetime experiences to come for me, typically involving traveling the world. When they said yes, I was elated. I knew nothing about the world outside of the US, but I would find out soon. My mom booked my flight on her credit card, using her points for half the cost. And just like that, the trajectory of my life had altered its course and taken flight.

That week in London was nothing short of amazing. It opened my eyes to the world. I saw my second Broadway play. (Who knew they had Broadway plays outside of New York?!) I quickly realized I was in one of the theater capitals of the world though. We bought tickets to see *Wicked* and everything from the production to the music and the choreography made the story come alive. The experience left me wanting more. So I figured how to get it.

I enrolled in my first study abroad program in London a little over a year later and found myself in an international student exchange program studying theater and global marketing. Taking in Shakespeare's *As You Like It* at the Globe Theatre where his plays were originally performed in 1599, discussing the impact of The Beatles, and listening to my marketing professor discuss Spotify, Europe's new innovative music platform. Believing him when he explained how it would never work in the United States because the system wouldn't allow it to succeed. (Man, was he wrong! The case study of Spotify, if one doesn't already exist, should be a tale of the people using technology to disrupt systems to benefit and cater to their evolving needs.) I was in a new world, where suddenly, I no longer worried about my survival. I worried about the skills needed to do business on an international scale, analyzing the impact of culturally sensitive marketing material and its power to make or break a product. I focused on living to the max during my semester abroad. Traveling to a new European country every weekend. It was the greatest escape.

I fell in love with flying. There is something about hovering over all the bullshit on the ground. My definition of when they go low, we go high. I could leave my troubles on the ground, even if it was only for a few hours. They didn't exist 30,000 feet in the air. So, my flights started getting longer and more frequent. Landing in a foreign country, where no one knew me, allowed me to be whomever I wanted to be and constructed my understanding of the world by absorbing as much culture as possible, leaving no room for me to think about the issues waiting for me back home. New experiences consumed my mind, and I wasn't thinking about past experiences or how far I'd come.

Studying theater in London was a natural fit for me. I was always on the stage. I loved performing and watching great performances. During my British theater class, we explored the entirety of the theater landscape, including performances for small audiences where we sat in a circle around the stage, up close and personal with the actors, as well as large-scale performances like *Thirty-nine Rooms*. My personal favorite, though, was *Death and The King's Horseman* by Wole Soyinka at London's Royal National Theater. The play takes place in Nigeria during British colonial rule, and it changed my view on what was possible with theater for Black artists.

My love for performance art comes from my upbringing. In my household, music was a staple. Culturally, we express ourselves through music. My dad is a huge music fan, which is evident since he named me after Stevie Wonder, and he used to wake my brother and me up every morning by blasting music throughout the house. It was part of his morning routine. We only had one bathroom, so we'd lay awake in our bunk beds waiting for him to be done before racing to be next in line. My dad was a DJ and had a short-lived rap career with a group of his friends. I love music but must admit that I have zero talent for it. The theater stage was always where I felt more comfortable expressing my artistic side. I always participated in school plays and in junior high school I had the opportunity to perform in an off-Broadway play that my class wrote and starred in, called *Get Out*. It was all about our wanting to get out of the hood and free ourselves from the constant danger and injustices we faced on a daily basis. I had a solo in which I performed a poem I wrote, and it made me comfortable with being on stage. So, getting the chance to explore theater in depth while in London was a great experience for me. A friend of mine recently posted the program from that show on Facebook, which included an additional poem that I wrote, titled "A Friendly Reminder." It brought me back to my mindset at fourteen years old. It read:

> All the thoughts jumbled in my head
> Come pouring down when I lay to bed
> I guess it's just a friendly reminder
> To organize myself like a three-ring binder.
> I'm not a saint, but I'm not a devil
> But my hard work is going to put me on a different level.
> People doing wrong is all I see
> I guess that's just a friendly reminder to just do me.*

*cues applause for my younger self. Reading this as an adult served as a friendly reminder to me that I've always used art and my words as a form of expression. It also put into context how long I've been fighting for myself.

My time living in London was inspiring. It was a new and interesting feeling, experiencing all the opportunities that were opening to me since taking the risky leap to attend Drexel given the extremely high cost. Here I was living in South Kensington, literally across the street from Kensington Palace, where Princess Diana lived, and a couple of blocks away from millionaire row. I'd walk outside my flat and my street would be lined with Bentleys, Maseratis, and a multitude of other exotic cars. One sunny spring morning, I was walking to class and saw a mom driving her young son to school in a purple Bentley convertible with the top down, wind blowing through her illustrious hair, seemingly carefree. As if the half-a-million-dollar car was the one she chose to drive that day just to celebrate the beginning of spring. I thought to myself, Wow I'm surrounded by wealth. And, apparently, I belong here.

I was in a new bubble, although at times I felt like I was an invited guest in someone else's bubble. Either way, I felt more alive than ever, and I didn't want it to end. I was hanging on by a thread though. The bubble was inflated to the max and ready to pop at any moment. My financial realities didn't measure up to my surroundings. Especially when at the time the British pound was about sixty cents to the US dollar. I did everything I could to stay afloat. Surviving on pasta or whatever cheap meal I could eat until my parents could send me more money. Trying to get them to understand the bubble and its importance to me exacerbated tensions between us, especially my father, something that often got lost in translation between me asking for money to keep the bubble afloat and their affordability to keep me in it. I was willing to do whatever it took to keep myself in the bubble with little regard to the reality outside of it. I couldn't afford its destruction. Reality often felt like this false construct though. Especially while I was entrenched in my bubble. But if I concerned myself with society's definition of reality, which often glorifies complacency over growth, I wouldn't have achieved anything. My dreams are my reality.

In hindsight, I realized that my time in London was lacking a sense of real community. Not from my cohorts but the environment overall. I wanted to have an experience living abroad where I could really immerse myself in the culture. I didn't realize how much more London had to offer until it was too late. I was visiting other countries almost every weekend while I was there with little time to truly explore the country I called home for a semester and live like the locals every day. When I first arrived in London, some of the students examined the curriculum and booked weekend getaways for almost every available weekend. I quickly jumped on the bandwagon and booked right along with them, spending most of my money in that first week with hopes that it would all work out. By that, I mean that my parents would help me out, and they reluctantly did, most of the time. Toward the end, they were done with me. In 2008, the US dollar didn't stretch very far compared to the British Pound and I was calling home for more money almost every week like clockwork. Traveling every week made me grow to hate tourist attractions. I wanted an experience where I would consistenly be amongst the locals. I did, however, develop strong relationships with my cohort. We all lived together in a co-ed flat, and we did almost everything together. The times we were in London, we enjoyed a lot. Exploring, going to dinners and pubs. I never liked beer until I went to London and a friend introduced me to Hoegaarden on tap. It was a light beer, but it was the gateway beer for me. The pub culture in London was so strong that I began drinking beer more and more until I started to really enjoy it, expanding my palate and understanding of its dynamic range of flavors.

One of the weekend trips we planned was to Italy, visiting Rome and Venice during an extended weekend. London's bank holidays offered us many extended weekends, which we took advantage of for the big trips. I fell in love with the culture and the strong sense of community in Rome. I was drawn to the calm, slow pace of their lifestyle that put beauty and preservation first. It took all of a day for me to decide I would come back at some point. After my semester in London, I returned to Drexel and signed up for Italian classes. I didn't have any direct plans to go back, but I knew I wanted to learn the language in case the opportunity ever arose.

RECESSION PROOF

I returned to Drexel after my semester abroad in London with my eyes wide open. I started to get a full picture of the world and how it operates. No matter what country I visited, no matter the differences in culture, there was always one constant: currency. After a semester of classes on campus at Drexel, it was time for me to apply for a new round of fall/winter co-op internships. I wanted to make sure I got something in the financial industry. I set my sights on getting an offer from a top firm, and I did just that, landing BlackRock, one of the leading investment management corporations in the world. As an analyst, I was tasked with reviewing all 300-plus of their mutual fund reports for accuracy before they were printed and sent to investors. It seemed like everything was going great. The bubble was flourishing, and I couldn't wait to start. I was making $17.50 an hour, and I felt like I was on top of the world, happy that this firm valued me enough to pay me that much as an intern. That was until other kids on co-ops kept revealing that they were making $26 to$30 an hour; regardless, I was eager to prove my value. Top firms also are known to pay less because of the value their name offers. I was excited when my first day arrived, kind of like the feeling you get on Christmas morning. It was Monday, September 15, 2008, and I was ready to walk into my future. However, my future had other plans. That was also the day that Lehman Brothers, one of the biggest US financial institutions, went belly up and the start of one of the worst recessions in modern history. That morning the over-inflated mortgage bubble had popped, and I was clueless as to what was in store for me when I arrived at the office. I woke up happy, got dressed, and made my way to the shuttle bus that would take me from Philadelphia to BlackRock's Delaware campus; I had no knowledge that this bubble had just popped and the world's financial markets were crumbling underneath us.

When I arrived at the office, I walked into pure chaos. It was like a scene out of a movie. Everyone was in a frenzy. Most of the employees had been there all weekend preparing for what was to come once markets opened that morning. I was thrown straight into the fire, and I had to learn quickly. There was little time for training as the uncertainty of everyone's jobs and future loomed overhead like a dark cloud. Vice presidents sat next to me calling their spouses to yank their kids out of school and get all their necessary doctor visits in, preparing for an anticipated termination, therefore revoking their health coverage. Associates were on the phone frantically calling to cancel their upcoming vacations because they needed to save as much as possible so they could stay in the too-expensive homes they would barely be able to afford. I saw people who worked for the company for twenty years get an email informing them that they no longer worked for the company. The worry and terror throughout the office over the following days and weeks as the markets continued to crash was contagious.

By the time Christmas rolled around, things were so scaled back, I'd really begun to question if this was the right path for me. BlackRock holiday parties were known to be legendary. Coworkers talked about how the year before the company arranged transportation and hotel stays for all employees in New York and had Maroon 5 perform. Photos couldn't do the decadence justice. But this recession year, some departments simply took their staff out for lunch. I understood the reasons, but I was also pissed. The money and the perks were the main reasons I wanted to go into finance. Now, as it seemed, there wasn't any of either. I sat at my desk every day thinking about how I never wanted to be in this position, especially as I started to see the very real effects of the recession beyond the office. Classmates were dropping out of school because their families couldn't afford it anymore. I saw students worry about their parents losing their childhood homes. It seemed like the only thing that was recession proof was tuition increases. It was scary to think that this could happen to anyone. Was I worthy enough to escape the same fate? I was already in debt and would be beholden to whatever high-paying job I could get. I needed to escape this fate by any means necessary. If I was going to be subjected to uncertainty and turbulence, then I needed to somehow be in control. I needed to create my own business. This was the spark that ignited my journey as an entrepreneur.

If there was one thing I knew I could count on, it was myself. I couldn't bring myself to think about finding love or starting a family until I felt I could provide a level of security that would be recession proof. The only thing I knew was that I never wanted to see that level of panic and fear in the eyes of my loved ones. I just couldn't do it. It may be a toxic masculine characteristic to want to be secure in what I could provide before making myself available to love, but it was how I felt. It was like I was fighting to escape the poverty I knew, only to see that there was another level of poverty that induced the same kind of stress. Going from poor to middle class and living check to check with little to spare after expenses is a kind of poverty I witnessed firsthand. There was no way I was working as hard as I was to make just enough. There's privilege in just enough, but I needed real money if I was going to make any kind of change in this world. I wanted wealth because I never wanted to be poor again. Suddenly, this path I was on didn't feel like an escape, no matter how good I was.

The ups and downs of my journey have taught me lessons about how my worth is not in my ability to provide but in my ability to bounce back and overcome challenges I'm faced with. It's one of the reasons I'm open to love now more than ever, even though I'm still broke—middle-class broke though, if that means anything. My experiences have allowed me to maneuver in and out of so many different bubbles, I've developed a skill for it in the form of resilience. My bubbles have always popped, often shattering my self-esteem, but that's a byproduct of change. Bubble pop, it's what they do. Surviving change comes at a cost though. I know now that I must nurture my self-esteem throughout the changes in my life. I want to have high self-esteem so that I can attract a woman with high self-esteem, and we can make babies that grow up to have high self-esteem. We will be a king and a queen raising kings and queens. It's something we can't just talk about; we have to do the work. But what makes a king anyway? And what's a king without resources?

There have been times when I've gone gallivanting in a foreign country, sleeping with beautiful women and feeling like king of the world. And times when I'm draped in designer threads, entertaining multiple women with money in my pocket, feeling like royal blood was flowing through my veins. But with age and wisdom came the realization that my behavior was that of a prince, not a king. I felt like I deserved the chance to be a prince though before feeling the weight of the world on my shoulders. I was forced to grow up to soon. Forced to be a man because of how society shoved the evils of this world in my face every day. I faced trauma just walking to school. My innocence was stripped from me early. Probably before I even made it to elementary school. And that was the product of my environment in the projects. I never got to relish the bubble of youth, because the bubble of survival was too strong to escape. But now I'm fully aware that my image, my being, is strong. And I know that when I emanate light I can break through any dark cloud formed against me.

WHEN THE UNTHINKABLE HAPPENS

In 2009, I needed to find an internship to begin the following semester, and competition was stiff for the top finance roles. Drexel was already fast-paced because our semesters were only ten weeks instead of the traditional fifteen weeks. Packing all the material we needed to learn into ten weeks was already insane and instead of the average fifteen to eighteen credits, I was maxed out with a twenty-one-credit course load. We had to secure all our interviews during midterm week, within the first five weeks, so time was a luxury I didn't have.

At the time I had a 3.7 GPA, so I didn't have any issues getting interviews. During midterm week, I not only had to prepare for six exams but I also had twelve co-op interviews, including multiple multi-hour interviews with top financial firms. It was a hectic week, but I was going on vacation with my family at the end of it, I just had to push through. We were set to go on a Caribbean cruise that we'd been planning for a year. I was looking forward to this vacation more than anything. Not only were my parents and brother going but my cousins Raylin and Coco as well as my aunt and uncle. I'd seen them all the weekend before our expected departure when I drove up to Harlem for Lehman Day, when everyone in our housing project complex got together, barbecued, and had fun to celebrate the community. I didn't live there anymore, but it's a tradition amongst all the housing projects in Harlem to host these days once a year, usually in the summer. I remember Raylin got into an altercation with someone during Lehman Day. I pulled him aside to try and calm him down and I pleaded with him to relax and think about the vacation we were going on next week. I told him to let this go so we could enjoy ourselves. "Think about how hard your mom worked to get to take you on this vacation." These would be some of my last words to him.

That Friday, at the end of midterm and interview week, I had my last two interviews, before needing to come home and pack to leave for our cruise. I woke up late that day and missed my first interview, which was scheduled at 9:00 a.m. At this point, I was sleep deprived as I had been running myself ragged that week and I guess my body knew I had to rest. I slept right through my alarm. When I woke up, I immediately sensed that something was off. There was this ominous feeling that came over me. It was more than just the frustration of waking up late and missing my interview. I had ten others that week, so I wasn't that upset. I was sure I had secured at least one or two of them. This feeling that I had was dark, and I didn't know what it was, but I got up and pressed on. I had another interview at JP Morgan that afternoon in Delaware and I rented a car to drive out there from Philly. It was a process that I had down to the minute I was set to leave for vacation. Meticulously Planning and organizing my time was key to getting everything I needed done.

After the interview, I got home and started to pack for our cruise. As I was packing, I got a call from my brother, who was hysterical, saying that Raylin had been shot, but he didn't know anything else yet. At first I couldn't comprehend what he was saying. The words he was saying weren't registering in my brain. Once I realized what he was telling me it was as if my world stopped. Immediately after, anger took over me. I thought it had something to do with the incident from the weekend before. I got angry at the thought of him not letting it go like I pleaded for him to do. So angry that I hung up on my brother and punched a hole in my bedroom wall. I was angry, but I never thought he wouldn't be ok. We'd been through so much, this was just something else we'd have to get through. A few minutes later my brother called me back to tell me that Raylin had been pronounced dead at the hospital.

I died that moment as well. Raylin was more than my cousin, he was my brother. We were only two and half weeks apart, both pisces, similar but different in many ways. He was the athletic, charming type that got along with everyone. I was more reserved, quiet, and nerdy. We balanced each other out in a lot of ways. We'd been in the same classroom together from pre-k through elementary school. And even when we weren't in the same school, we saw each other every day. Always meeting at my grandfathers house in Lehman Village projects after school. We celebrated our birthdays together almost every year. He was the person I knew I could always count on to be there for me when I needed, and vice versa, no questions asked. Losing that kind of bond, was and still is devestating. We were 21 when he was killed. I'd seen this kind of tragic scene play out many times before in East Harlem, but I never imagined it would happen to my family. We were flawed, often in survival mode, but definitely not deserving of something like this. I knew we would never be the same again.

I couldn't do anything in that moment after my brother told me he was gone. Here I was in my room packing for a vacation, now I had to figure out what to do next. I lived in a townhouse in west Philly three classmates and our friends were always at our house. I remember walking downstairs seeing everyone in the living room watching tv, having fun, and I just had to spit out what just happened. And without a second thought, they rallied for me. Rakita, Amanda, Adam, Ron, Devin, Tiara, Giselle, Everic. From helping me pack, to returning my rental car I'd had for my interview, and getting me to the bus to get to New York and to my family. I'm incredibly grateful to have had them in my corner. I was in a daze of disbelief and I thank God they were there to help me through it. As soon as I got off the bus at 34th street, I took a cab to the hospital where there were dozens of people outside. It felt sureal. No one knew what to do. Friends and family was there to support us but it didn't matter. It's a day I'll never forget.

I spent about two weeks in New York with my family mourning Raylin's death. The funeral was the toughest part. Seeing him in that casket changed something within me. Hearing all the cries and the screams. Seeing my aunt being unable to even walk in the church. It was all so heartbreaking. It was one of the hardest things I'd ever have to do. And then I had to go back to school. Drexel's ten-week semesters left no time for mourning the way I would have liked. I had finals and had to catch up on the two weeks of material I missed in all six of my classes. I had too much riding on this. I couldn't fail a class because that would throw my whole plan off. I had my classes planned out down to a single credit in order to graduate with all three of my major concentrations, and my professors would not give me an extension. They let me know that if I missed the final, I would get an F in the class. I hated myself for leaving my family and

I felt like I was abandoning them. I couldn't face them. Mostly because Raylin's loyalty to his family is what had cost him his life. He was only in the situation he was in because one of our third cousins called him and asked him to help with his situation. And here I was, not willing to give up mine. But I channeled those feelings to fuel the wildfire within me. There had to be a reason for all this, right? I'm not named after legends for nothing. I had to continue to grow stronger and faster. I had to find what that reason was. But sadness was the dirt and water that was trying to put out my fire. I couldn't allow it. So, I tried my best to suppress my sadness and anger and only acknowledged it when it was too strong for me to fight off. Not knowing that supressing these feelings was manifesting depression and anxiety that would eventually show up.

These battles were a declaration of war between who I was versus who I wanted to be. Suppressing my negative emotions became a top defense strategy for who I wanted to be. This strategy won a lot of battles, but I began to wonder if my reality would win the war. Could anyone tell how truly angry and sad I was inside? How would they react if they found out? I couldn't let that happen. I was surrounded by people who seemingly had no struggles. I didn't want to become the person known for having problems because it wasn't anyone's business but mine. I didn't want to become the stereotype of the angry Black man from the hood who couldn't make it at a predominantly white school. It was bad enough being the only Black person in my classes, wondering if everyone was wondering how I got there: Was it affirmative action? Was it merit-based? If so, is he even smart? I started to care what people thought about me, so I did what I had become so deft at: I went after as much as I could. I moved so fast that the sadness, anger, and opinions of others couldn't catch up. But the depression and anxiety played the waiting game. Its strategy was patience and it knew what I didn't. Eventually, I had to stop running because at some point I would wear myself out. And when I did, it would be ready to attack. My strategy for who I wanted to be had its side effects. I didn't let anyone get too close to me and kept everyone at a distance. Any romantic relationship I entered was sabotaged once it got too serious. If they ever really knew me, they'd know how angry and sad I was. How would that affect the person I wanted to become? I couldn't hand that power over to anyone. I wouldn't let myself.

RETURNED TO SENDER: LETTERS TO SOULS IN THE HEREAFTER

Dear Raylin,

I miss you like crazy. It's been over ten years since you've left us, and I still think about you often. To this day I haven't come across anyone who's looked out for me the way you did. Growing up in the hood as the geeky, asthmatic kid wasn't easy, and you always had my back, sticking up for me on the playground in elementary school or on the block, making sure no one fucked with me. I still remember that time when we were in high school, and I had that beef with one of the Dominican students at my school. When I texted you to let you know that I was going to fight after school, I had no idea that you immediately started working to gather soldiers on my behalf. But I was glad to see you and the army you led when I walked out of that school building at 3:00. How you rallied all those people in such a short amount of time to come to protect me and make sure I wouldn't get jumped is a testament to who you were. A leader who would do anything for the people you loved. It's what I always admired most about you. But you were way more than just my protector. You always pushed me to be a better me. Something I took for granted. You were the most charming and loyal person I've ever known. And at the time of your death, I wasn't fully present in my realization of how much I needed you. I was so focused on pushing our mission forward. Or at least holding up my end of the bargain. I think that's why I got so angry when I found out you were gone. I didn't even know what happened yet, but I knew that you had not held up your end because you were no longer here to see it through. I still feel guilty about that initial reaction. I was so laser focused on our vision of world domination. Between my education and your street smarts, we were poised to create something great. And at that moment, my mind couldn't reconcile this new reality. And when the anger subsided and the sorrow swooped in, I couldn't find a way to forgive myself. The only thing I could do was double down on my end of the deal.

And I've gotten pretty far along. I know you'd be proud of me if you were still alive. But I have to admit that I'm having trouble completing the mission in this new reality. I'm sure you know that Coco has passed. I'd like to think that you two are together, but I struggle with finding the strength I need to keep going without her, without both of you. I don't want to let you down, I don't want to let me down, I don't want to let anyone down. But it's taking a lot longer than we anticipated. Who knew it would be this difficult? I only wish that you were here to help talk me through it. Like old times. When you pushed me to be great. Your cheers always made me feel comfortable walking into the unknown. Without them, I'm feeling a little lost. I'm finding my way back though. Slowly, but surely.

I think what I'll miss the most is celebrating our birthdays together. We were Pisces twins with big dreams for our futures. We celebrated almost every birthday together until we were twenty-one, the last year of your life, and every birthday since hasn't been the same. I've always tried to overcompensate for that missing piece by trying to have a big birthday. People today are still talking about my twenty-fifth, when I rented out a private room at Beauty & Essex in the Lower East Side. It was epic, in a fashion I know you would have approved.

I don't regret having grown apart from you in those last years. No one could foresee this coming, and we were both focused on our respective paths. It was all part of the plan. But as time goes on, and memories fade, the only thing I regret is not having held on to your words harder. Not having permanently stored our myriad of conversations in my brain. Not having been more present in your presence. But alas, I must come to terms with the things I can't change, as they say.

I remember that summer day in 2009 when you were killed in Harlem like it was yesterday. The place that we loved so much had taken you from our family, and it was truly unbelievable. I was in Philadelphia at the time, away at school, but my mind replays with a clarity of an eyewitness the image of you running for your life, to be shot in the back, bleeding out on the corner of 125th Street and Amsterdam Avenue. To this day, I can't walk by that street unfazed, usually trying my best to avoid it. I know the circumstances around your death can and have been debated, but that white man who killed you in an unnecessary attempt at revenge, after your botched robbery attempt, was wrong. You both were, but he took it too far. You were unarmed, and it kills me that you'll never get the justice you deserve, a fact that was very hard for me to internalize. Especially since the man who killed you received a medal for his "heroic" act. An act that was, in my opinion, extremely cowardly. But the media and the irresponsible reporting on the deaths of Black men always painted a picture of us that resembled monsters more than humans, with little to no regard to perils we face when gentrifiers come into our neighborhoods, trying to assert control. But know that none of that mattered to me. I know the truth, that you died being you. Fiercely loyal to your family and showing up when they called. The admiration and honor in that is how I choose to remember you, but it was hard to get to this point. I held in a lot of hate for everyone who was involved, who was still breathing. As well as a deep sadness at the fact that I'd never get the chance to talk to you again.

I never fully realized how much I held in until seven years later when I found myself having a mental breakdown, uncontrollably crying on my parents' basement floor for hours. I didn't just miss you; I was still in pain. I knew at that moment that I needed help and I had to seek therapy. I'd recently been laid off from an amazing job and I was questioning my worthiness, questioning everything. And that's how my journey of healing began, although it wouldn't be until a year later when I was in a job with good enough insurance where I could afford the best therapist I could find. I was very fortunate enough to find a Black man who had a PhD in psychotherapy from top schools, all things that were very important to me. I don't believe I would have the success that I had if my therapist wasn't a Black man, an extremely intelligent and skilled one at that. It would still take me a couple of months before I would really start to be comfortable enough to open myself up. But I started to feel the effects immediately. I started to feel closer to myself as an individual. I know that's what you would want for me, but it's still hard to let you go.

When you passed, there was a petition that your mom started to get justice for you. I wanted justice, but I hated doing it in such a public forum, asking for help. I never thought it would be our family dominating news cycles in such a nega-tive way. Your story became a *Law and Order* episode though. I couldn't believe it when I first heard. But then again, it was in true Raylin fashion. I hated the story that was being portrayed about you. I knew it wasn't true, but what about people who didn't know you? As much as I wanted justice, I didn't want to promote it, I didn't want that story to be your legacy. But I did it anyway. I wasn't strong enough to stand in my convictions. I wasn't completely sure if I was right or not. I didn't have much experience in what to do with this kind of loss, with this kind of attention. I struggled with figuring it out. Should I just do what everyone else tells me to do? To continue like normal? I felt like I was way too young and inexperienced to confidently answer all the questions I had. And you know we didn't talk about things like this in our family. The confu-sion made me feel like no one understood what I was going through. I couldn't relate to anyone. People just kept saying, "Be strong." So, I stopped trying to come up with answers to all the questions I had. I hid them from myself so I wouldn't have to face them. It seemed like that's what all the strong people were doing. But eventually, my mind ran out of hiding places and running from myself became a defense strategy. But it was exhausting. I needed help with strategies to overcome this because I didn't feel strong. Which is one of the reasons I decided to try psychotherapy. Therapy for me was the process of realizing that asking myself the hard questions and facing my honest answers is what strength actually looks like. I wish more than anything you were here to witness this version of me. But your peaceful rest is more important to me than anything. Until we meet again, King.

Love Always,
Your Forever Best Man.

IN PURSUIT OF SAFETY

Work, work, work, and more work. In America, we're told the harder we work, the more rewards we'll see. And that if our dreams don't come true, then it's because we're not working hard enough. For most of my life I believed this to be true. I equated work ethic with survival. Taking on as much as I could hoping that one day all that hard work would pay off. But all that "grinding" and "hustling' actually took more from me than it provided. It robbed me of my innocence, time, love, etc. For as long as I can remember I always operated from a place of meeting a goal that would either help me survive or put me in a position to survive. I don't know how it feels to not have a goal in mind for a greater vision of my life. America todays has this way of dangling opportunity in your face only to move the goal post everytime your close to grasping it.

When I was young, I wanted to be a lawyer. I had no clue what a lawyer did. It was just an image of success, safety, and stability. It wasn't until I worked in a law firm for a year that I realized I didn't want to be a lawyer. I'd gotten a few offers from the twelve interviews I went on during the week that Raylin passed. I chose to do my co-op at Blank Rome, LLP, a top law firm in Philadelphia and New York. I worked as a marketing analyst, and the experience served as a way for me to conduct reconnaissance in the field. I was able to see if I wanted to become a lawyer and I gained insight into what that life was like before committing to law school. The job was fun and challenging but less intense and competitive than a job in finance. It had only been a month since Raylin passed when I had to start at Blank Rome, and I didn't have it in me to be in a cutthroat environment. With Blank Rome, I got to work in both of their offices, sometimes spending weeks at a time back home in New York with my family. Their office was in the famed Chrysler Building, and it was my first time being in the building. The dream was continuing. Although the pay was a lot less than a finance role, I loved the work I was doing and I got to plan huge events, including their industry-leading clean energy conference at the Natural Museum of Science in Philadelphia. I also got an inside look into creating proposals for business, one time hand-delivering a proposal to a top energy executive at Sunoco. Although co-ops were only six months full time, the team kept me on for an additional six months part-time while I was taking classes leading up to my senior year at Drexel.

Being up close and personal with lawyers, I quickly recognized that it wasn't as glamorous as some of the characters I grew up watching made it seem, like Claire Huxtable from The Cosby Show. Instead, I saw depression and overall unhappiness. I fostered some good relationships with the attorneys as they always came to me for promotional items to send to clients. They all advised me not to go into law based on what I wanted to do. I wanted an exciting life; I didn't want to be chained to a desk reading all the time. The safety and stability that came with being a lawyer were a driver for me. That and the excitement and money I thought it'd bring. I didn't know any lawyers, they didn't come from where I'm from. I romanticized the profession from what I'd personally seen in the media. But wanting what I saw was enough to keep me out of trouble growing up in East Harlem. I'd heard somewhere that if I was ever arrested, I wouldn't be able to be a lawyer as it would go on my permanent record and follow me for the rest of my life. his frightened me enough to unlock a level of survival mode that would stay with me throughout my childhood. Especially since it seemed like everyone around me was getting arrested. It was the norm, the police was everywhere. It was like constantly walking on the edge of a cliff, especially with the New York Police Department's mandate from the war on drugs that had cops infiltrating our neighborhood and patrolling every corner hunting Black men and ruining many innocent lives. They constantly berated us and interrupted our family gatherings with the threat of use of force if we didn't cooperate. Our rights never seemed to matter to them. But I knew I had a right to dream, and I refused to allow them to ruin my future or my dream of being a lawyer. I couldn't hand them that much power and autonomy over my well-being.

When I think about it, this is how I started to develop my isolating behavior. Even when I was physically present, often my mind wasn't. When I was with a group of other kids going around Harlem "wilding," because we were frustrated by our forced limitations and craved a sense of freedom, I was too busy making sure I didn't get caught. I had a mission and I wouldn't let anyone deter me from it. To protect myself, I created my own bubble. I wasn't going to allow anyone to get me arrested or killed by police or a rival project or gang. I was always thinking ahead and creating plans and contingency plans that would ensure my safety. And the risks didn't matter. Part of surviving in East Harlem in the '90s and early 2000s was showing up and being known in your hood so no one would mess with you. I was always outside, so it was easy to get caught up in what others around me was doing. I stayed out the way a lot, but if the group of people I was around went out looking for trouble, even if I was uneasy about, if I felt like I had no other choice, I was rolling with the group. But I would never let anyone or anything, impede the prioritization of my safety. Danger was all around me. I couldn't avoid it, but I could avoid puting my body directly in front of it.

The NYPD caused a lot of anxiety for me. Black boys were being hunted by cops who never saw humanity in us. In their eyes, we were a threat to be neutralized. That thought consumed me, trying not to get stopped and frisked and knowing that if a cop decided to plant something on me (which they often did to others, one time to my younger brother Jordin), it would be my word against theirs, and the justice system never believed Black boys. The system made sure we knew our word meant nothing against the word of the police. No matter how corrupt and racist they were, the city gave them complete power over us. They had the ability to end my life in many ways, from putting an arrest on my record that would impede future job prospects to actually locking me up with fabricated charges. It fueled my desire to stay out of trouble when there was potential trouble all around me. It's how the system was designed, to keep us within our four-block radius so the only option is to rebel. This created the justification for a police presence so they could find any excuse to lock us up. It's a vicious cycle that instills feelings of a lack of self-worth, and that our voices didn't matter.

Today, in the pursuit of safety for our community, we see criminal justice reform discussions typically mention the war on drugs from a policy view. Rarely do I see enough talk about the damage the war left in its wake: the human effects, both physical and psychological. I've witnessed the toll it took on us and I live it everyday. It breaks up families, causes mental health issues, and keeps us dependent on a system that doesn't care to see us thrive. Having "successfully" navigated through, I feel a sense of duty to not let us be forgotten. To not let the egregious acts our government committed against us be swept under the rug. The war on drugs is a policy title. But if we're calling a spade a spade, it was really a war on Black people. State-sanctioned genocide against its own citizens. They expect their terror against us will cause us to surrender, but I know I never will. I'm just not built that way. I'll never stop fighting. I've learned that I have as much a right to thrive in this country as anyone else. And I want every Black person in America to know that as well. We have to stand up for ourselves and our rights.

It's important for our leaders to not be afraid to admit that the amount of injustice and inequity that Black men and women face daily far exceeds the inequity white women and men face. Our criminal justice system is just slavery by a different name. Fueled by the majority white owned private prisons. They come into our neighborhoods, round us up, throw us in cages, and then force us to do low-wage labor. Even in so called progressive states like California, prisoners are often used to battle treacherous wildfires that are exacerbated by climate change at the hands of wealthy. Paying $2 to $5 per day to clean up their mess while they rake in billions, with only an extra $1 if they end up in the fire, and time off their sentence. Reports estimate this program saves California an estimated $90 million to $100 million per year. Instead of paying market rate for this dangerous job and reducing the state's police budget by $90 million to $100 million, the government of California chosses slavery. It's all strategically designed, and it aids the genocide of Black men.

By continuing to promote archaic and fabricated views of Black terror and inferiority, the system justifies the need for police presence in Black neighborhoods. But what we need is resources and the ability to flourish without the threat of violence if we do. E.G. Black Wall Street. Part of the reason I'm writing this book is to try and take back control of our narrative. To dispell the images in the media which constantly pushes false narratives of issues like Black-on-Black crime, as if crime is not based on proximity and opportunity, regardless of race. Especially when statistically, white people are responsible for most of the crime in the US. In 2016, the US Justice Department reported that of the total 8.4 million crimes that year, 69.56 percent were committed by a white person. It makes me frustrated to think about this because we don't hear about the magnitude of white crime from media outlets who push their agendas first, agendas set by their wealthy owners. Even the concept of "white-collar crime" is just marketing created to portray white crime as something acceptable, while a Black person who commits a small crime to try and feed their child is marketed as unacceptable and monstrous. Everyone bears a responsibility regarding the narratives they push. My hope is to challenge readers to not accept the status quo. To question everything. And if you're in a position of power, use that power to change the system for good.

This pursuit of safety made me hate authority. It's why I feel more comfortable in entrepreneurial and/or managerial positions; I don't like the idea of someone else having control over my well-being. My mind is not wired to receive it positively. My whole life I've been told what I can and can't do with my body. And as soon as I broke out of the box, there was no way I was going back. The school-to-prison pipeline makes going to school feel like training for prison. It often felt like there was more focus on obedience and behavior than actual learning. Since I was in kindergarten, I was told how to sit, when to speak, to walk the halls in a line up by size order, etc. Even sitting still couldn't just be sitting still. We had to have our fingers crossed at all times and a form of punishment usually followed right after if we ever dared to disobey. Our bodies were not our own. Our minds were not our own, and I hated it. And what made it worse is that everyoen accepted this as the norm.

When I got to high school, I had my first taste of freedom and got swept away by it. It was the first time I didn't have to wear a uniform, and we could come and go as we pleased, with the right to leave campus during lunch and go anywhere we wanted in the allotted time period. But as a freshman, not knowing how to manage this newfound freedom, I took advantage of it. It wasn't out of the norm for me to miss my first-period class or take three consecutive lunch periods instead of only my assigned one. I often hung out on the corner with friends or in the lunchroom playing Spades. But at some point, toward the end of my freshman year, I realized I was doing myself a disservice. With my new freedom came a responsibility, and I wasn't holding up my end of the bargain. My parents didn't play when it came to school. I also had some good teachers who realized my potential and helped me see that I could do and be more. But my body still didn't feel like my own. Authority still loomed over my head, mostly from my father whose way of disciplining me often included a lot of yelling, which was the worst for me. My mind couldn't take it. I would shut down as a defense mechanism whenever he raised his voice. Because here I was, not able to be myself, even at home. Instead, I had to be a version of myself that appeased authority.

I didn't know how to express my feelings at the time, so I often shut down and let the stress of my lack of freedom stack up and overflow with anger. I couldn't properly articulate what I needed for my growth, and my dad couldn't articulate what he needed from me. So, we'd often get into fights. A couple of which escalated to physical. Because neither one of us knew how to properly communicate our feelings and needs. Once I even packed a bag and left. I think my dad thought I was spoiled and disobeying him. But I'm realizing now, that I didn't feel safe in that moment and I had to leave. I've always had the utmost respect for my dad, but he projected a lot of his environment on me. And I didn't know how to prove to him I could be trusted. That I wasn't like the inmates he patroled on Rikers Island as a Corrections Officer. Often his discipline felt like he didn't trust me to do the right things, and that felt like a betrayal. It took me a long time to realize how much it wasn't. Discipline as a parenting method and submission for the sake of submission is a concept that was handed down to him. He embraced it and continued to pursue that concept through the deference structure of the military as if we were in teh Navy. We clashed not out of disdain for each other or a lack of love, but a lack of knowledge. He didn't have a rule book on how to discipline a freedom-loving, authority-hating child. He doubled down on what he knew. What kept him out of trouble.

Part of the anger and betrayal that I felt toward him as a teen was because I didn't understand why he didn't get it. I was angry that he didn't know me well enough to understand me and felt betrayed every time I wanted him to take the time to learn, and he didn't. What we wanted and needed from each other at times seemed so different. It often left me feeling like I was a constant disappointment. I tried so hard to succeed on my own, to prove to him that I could be successful, doing it the way I envisioned. But it often felt like every success was preceded by a mountain of disappointment and failure that drowned it out, like choosing the college I wanted to go to but not getting enough money to go and needing him to help, even though I knew he didn't want to. It made me fear failure because it brought on anxiety in having to admit that I didn't have all the answers or ask for help. My ego couldn't take it, which meant I had to do something bigger. I think men who grow up with their dads in the household are driven by a desire to prove themselves to their dads, to be able to break away and stand on their own two feet. It's the example we see from our dads that help mold us. Which is why it's so imperative that the black family structure sticks together. Because no one has ever made it anywhere alone. Before this healing process, my brain didn't have the capacity for authority from others. Accepting power dynamics in which I was powerless never felt right to me. I didn't even like that my own father had power over me, I definitely can't give it to someone else voluntarily. For my safety.

INTERLUDE:
SAFETY IN AMERICA FOR A BLACK MAN

Imagine you've found yourself suddenly in life-threating danger. Would your first thought be to call the police? Would you feel relief once they showed up?

If you can relate to these sentiments, if you've ever felt comfortable calling those whose job it is to protect and serve you, then you can never imagine how it feels to be a Black man in America. To have the people who supposed to keep you safe, be a leading cause of death for everyone that looks like you.

How could we ever really feel safe?

Now beyond emotions and feelings. Imagine your protectors going on the offensive and running massive plays to attack you in order to fulfill their mission of causing the demise of everyone that looks like you.

I know what you're thinking. How could your protection be the thing that attacks you? Hypocrisy.

Safety is a privilege. Protection is a luxury.

Survival mode shouldn't be a permanent state. But as Black men, we have permanent targets on our backs. And rarely do we get twenty-four hours to live without being reminded of those targets.

Freedom has been redefined. Again.
But I wonder if, in the land of the free, we were ever actually free? It all sounds like carefully curated propaganda. The greatest marketing strategy in the world. Politics in action.

I can't think of a single time in American history when everyone was equally free.

It's a hard pill to swallow. Especially when we're looked at as the blueprint to freedom.

There's a great quote that says when you are accustomed to privilege, equality looks like oppression.

It's why when we say Black Lives Matter so that the police won't kill us, those who are used to the privilege of safety by the police think we're trying to attack them. No.
As Americans, we deserve the privilege of safety in the country we built.

The treatment of Black men in America exacerbates the lugubrious state of humanity.

And yet, we persevere. We keep moving. Just like the legendary Black men I'm named after.

Being in the presence of other Black men is when I feel the safest. When I can let my guard down and be me. We are our brothers' keepers.

Thank you for this luxurious privilege.

ASK AND YOU MIGHT RECEIVE

My ability to overcome loss stems from learning how to ask for help when I needed it. Becoming comfortable with tapping into my network has put me in situations that allowed me to use resources I might not have had access to otherwise. One notable example of this was the summer before my senior year at Drexel. I was worried about financing my upcoming semester abroad in Italy when I lost my largest scholarship. It was $11,000. All of a sudden, it was gone, and I had no way of making that up. I did everything I could to find the money, exhausting all my options. I lobbied the financial-aid office, sent appeals, anything to try and raise the funds I needed. I was maxed out on loans and had already committed additional funds to fees for my study abroad program in Italy. The stress was overwhelming as I was also in the middle of my course load and had to finish everything two weeks ahead of the already fast-paced ten-week curriculum—and I was still working part-time at Blank Rome, LLP. I was scared that in the fourth quarter I was going to have to give up everything and go home with no degree and a bunch of debt, like so many others before me at Drexel, which was once deemed the most expensive university in America. But that was not an option for me. I had worked too hard to get to where I was, and there was no way I was going to let $11,000 stop me from completing my last year of school. I had to find a solution, so I began to think about how to raise funds from unconventional sources.

In the fourth grade, my teacher Mr. Pantelidis, a white man and one of the strictest I've ever had, would always proclaim, "Close, but no cigar," whenever someone in the class got an answer wrong. It took me until my adult years to understand this phrase, but I understood from its context that it meant you were wrong. To me, it was just an arcane white person's idiom that was out of touch for a classroom full of Black fourth graders. Culturally it was hard to relate to my white teachers growing up. Even though my community was majority black, most of my teachers were white and their culture was foreign to me. But phrases like this one stuck with me. Mr. Pantelidis drilled it into us and instilled a sense of fear of getting a wrong answer. It made me hate the idea of coming close but not making it. The wasted effort and the humiliation of not making the cut always bugged me. I never wanted to hear or be associated with that phrase ever again. It's like when Brandy, one of the greatest artists of all time, told us, "Almost doesn't count!" I feared that "almost," especially when it came to graduating college. I couldn't take the idea of being the guy who almost got a degree. Whenever my back was against the wall, all I could do was hear was Mr. Pantelidis saying, "Close, but no cigar!" I knew that jobs didn't care if you almost graduated. Either you have a degree or you don't. More importantly, I didn't want to be an almost Drexel graduate. I'd seen it happen too many times and, to be honest, I was in too deep. As much as my father preached to me, "This school is too expensive, go to BMCC [Borough of Manhattan Community College]," I just couldn't do it. In fact, it made me want to succeed even more. I was close, I had to get the cigar by any means necessary, even if it meant going into six-figure debt. Admittedly though, I had no idea how taking on that debt would impact my life. Before the 2008 recession, all signs pointed to me graduating with a high-paying job. But even after the economy shifted, I couldn't back down. The thought never entered my mind.

I needed to exhaust all my options before throwing in the towel on finding the $11,000 for my fifth and final year at Drexel. As President of DMAP, I developed a relationship with our faculty advisor who helped us navigate operations. He just so happened to be the Chief Financial Officer at Drexel, and a Black man. All my dealings with him had been about the business of DMAP, so the thought of going to him for personal reasons never really crossed my mind. This was until I had no other choice but to expand my reach of possibilities. I requested a meeting with him and told him about my situation. The meeting went well and ended with him telling me he'd see what he could do. I left the main building excited about the possibility but worried because I didn't get a definitive yes. As I walked across campus to my car, all I could think about was figuring out a plan Z in case this didn't come through.

As soon as I got to my car, I heard a notification from my phone indicating I had a new email. I opened my car door but decided to look at the email before getting in, in case I needed to stay on campus for a while. When I opened my email, I was stunned to see that my tuition balance had been paid off. The amount of joy and relief I felt in that moment was overwhelming. But more than anything, I was even more fired up about the path I was on and knew that I would pay it forward in any way that I could. I was also very proud of myself for not giving up. I was honestly a couple of days away from calling it quits and giving up everything. Experiences like this helped me to be OK with the fact that sometimes losing is a part of life. It's giving up that I can't fade, though. To me, giving up feels like death. It's the pressure that I put on myself to succeed at all costs that made giving up feel like a betrayal. Reflecting on these instances has helped me realize that every time I've experienced loss, I was able to become whole again as long as I didn't give up. And it's been the times when my back has been against the wall that I found a way to overcome and know what I was truly made of. It's the beauty of my struggle that makes me worthy of all the blessings I receive. I just need to make sure I never forget it.

ISLAND HOPPING OFF THE AMALFI COAST

I was feeling run down from the work at the law firm Blank Rome LLP, my huge course load at Drexel, and the emotional toll of Raylin's passing. I needed an escape. I'd started taking Italian classes when I got back from London and after three semesters of Italian, Drexel announced a new study-abroad opportunity at the beginning of what would be my senior year, fall 2010. It was an immersive semester in Italy at the American University of Rome. The prerequisites just happened to be three semesters of Italian; it was meant to be. The program fee was $5,000, and I definitely didn't have it. I decided to ask the Chief Marketing Officer at Blank Rome to pay the $5,000 program fee for me in exchange for some additional marketing work. All signs pointed to them paying the fee. I confirmed my attendance in the program and was ready to go but, at the last minute, the firm decided they would not pay my fee. I had a choice to make. Either drop out or take on more debt. I decided on the latter. This was the loan that maxed me out before I found out about the loss of my scholarship. I was already up to my neck in debt, but I couldn't let this once-in-a-lifetime opportunity pass. But really, I needed the escape by any means necessary.

Being in a foreign land and able to speak the language with locals blew up a different kind of bubble for me. I was living amongst Roman locals in the residential area of Trastevere where basal amenities that were custom in the US now proved to be a luxury we weren't afforded. None of that mattered though; it was still the time of my life. Pizza Boom, a small pizza shop right under my apartment, where I could buy pizza by the square, was the best pizza I'd ever eaten. It was better than all the restaurants near the tourist areas of Rome and better than anything I've had in New York City. I always stopped there before or after class, depending on the day. Our campus was small but had a great community feel. In addition to continuing my Italian studies, the majority of my other classes focused on international relations. I studied the global landscape from the perspective of international economic and trade organizations such as the International Monetary Fund and the World Bank. I studied their organizational structures and how they operated both internally and with participating countries they served. International trade, though, was probably one of the hardest concepts for me to grasp, at least the quantitative aspects of it. But once I got it, I naturally excelled. These studies helped me see how truly global our modern society is. Understanding international trade on a macro and micro level helped me put context to just how scarce the worlds resources are and how important it is for Black people to get more involved in global operations for the sake of our survival. Coming from Harlem, where my worries focused on making sure I didn't cross the wrong street or how I could get the new Jordans, it was a proud feeling to shift my mindset to how money and aid were being funneled to "Third World" countries, and if the produce I was eating came from abroad due to an agreement someone created with another country.

The simplicity of life in Rome is what I loved the most. After class, I could take a short walk to the Trevi Fountain for the best gelato in the world. Then head home, stopping first for a good bottle of wine, which probably didn't cost more than five euros. What more could I want? I had needed an escape, and this was the best one I could ask for. I visited Tuscan Vineyards for wine tasting and pasta making. I partied solo in Florence, where I got attacked by bedbugs from the hostel I was staying in, not noticing until I was on the train back to Rome. I island-hopped off the Amalfi Coast with a large group of my classmates, driving through Italy to Sorrento before embarking on boat rides to Capri and Positano. We hiked up mountainous terrain to arrive in the town of Capri first, rewarding ourselves with delicious limoncello drinks when we arrived at the top, taking in the vast views of the Mediterranean that appeared to us, surprisingly, after every turn. Lunch in Capri with a group of friends is probably one of my top five experiences. The beauty and ease echoed a lifestyle that I knew I could get used to.

Positano was our next adventure, and we'd also have to trek to make our way to the "famed" black sand beaches. We were all hungry and exhausted by the time we arrived, and I saw a deli and got ecstatic. I thought I could get a taste of home. I ended up having one of the best turkey heros I've ever had, much better than the turkey heros I used to buy for lunch every morning in elementary school from the corner deli in Harlem. The fresh turkey and freshly baked bread left a lasting impression on me. The black sand beaches were aesthetically pleasing too. Beautiful to look at but extremely uncomfortable due to the rocky sand. I vowed that whenever I returned, it would be to dock my yacht in the crystal-clear water and admire the view. It appeared that was the thing to do on the Amalfi Coast. We took a boat ride around the coast and through the blue grotto, a majestic cave that you'd have to see to believe. Before entering, we stopped by the entrance of the cave and our guide told us to look down. It was the clearest water I'd ever seen, with green reflections from the sea life on the ocean floor and small calm waves that glistened off the rays of the sun with each crash. There was a large rock formation beneath us, and I stuck my hand in the water to touch it before our guide quickly informed us that the rock was actually over thirty feet below us. The water was so clear, the ocean floor appeared as if it was within arm's reach.

We stopped in Pompei on our drive back to Rome. A once thriving city in 79 A.D. destroyed by a volcano and preserved for centuries. As I took in the vastness of the destruction, I wondered if we would be doomed to a similar fate, with future generations of humans visiting museums of destroyed skyscrapers. Would our current way of life be preserved to honor the time and remind those future generations of just how fragile life can be? History shows us how so many life altering moments has been out of our control, with mother nature having the last say. And yet we continue to tempt fate. Causing climate change and accelerating destruction for the sake of capital. I fell in love with Italy because its beauty didn't lie in luxury or material things but in community and a deep connection to its past. The way they preserved and honored their history was more foreign to me than the language. I fell in love with that aspect of its culture. Probably because as a Black American, I never felt connected to any historical aspect of my ancestry other than slavery, which feels like it's being erased from history every day. But this bubble was glorious. Imperfect, but I loved it. Outside of the bubble was grief hovering overhead, waiting for its moment to break in and overtake my mind. I couldn't allow that to happen.

FROM GHANA WITH LOVE

While studying abroad in Italy, I took two really big trips to Africa. The first was my trip to Morocco, where I spent a week with two of my classmates who were also studying abroad with me. The other was when the semester ended, when I spent three weeks in Ghana during the Christmas 2010 break. The main reason for my trip was to volunteer at an orphanage that was owned and operated by my friend Ama's mother. It was a culturally immersive experience for me, to say the least. At the time, Ghana wasn't as developed as other countries I'd visited, but it had its own magic that can't be replicated anywhere else. We were there on a mission to be of some help. This trip turned out to be an experiment in duality. We helped out with the orphanage, but we also partied like rock stars and took in historical sites like the Cape Coast Castle where our ancestors were sent to be shipped off to be sold to the highest bidder. I stood in old stone dungeons where enslavers would shackle and hold hundreds of captured Africans. The dungeons had linear grooves dug into the ground which acted as a makeshift plumbing system because the captured Africans weren't allowed the decency of a bathroom. Imagine being squuezed into a crowded room where everyone had to go on themselves and there was nothing but grooves in the floor to try and flush it away. But in reality there was no escaping it. I could feel the sorrow in the room. I could feel the weight of our ancestors. In that moment, I understood firsthand how we were relegated to less than human. I felt the fear, stress, anxiety, shame, and hopelessness that our ancestors had to endure. But walking through the "Door of No Return" hit me like a ton of bricks, experiencing for a moment how truly frightening it must've been. Beyond the door, all you could see is the endless ocean. I imagined having to cope with the uncertainty of it all. Surviving every day not knowing what horrors the next day would bring. I felt the energy of their pain.

I believe that this ability to cope with uncertainty is encoded in Black people's DNA. The drive to survive against all odds, no matter how difficult or traumatic, is a characteristic passed down from generation to generation. However, we're in a time where survival has become the bare minimum. Surviving is the least we can do to honor our ancestors. They survived so we can thrive. It's why my goals now look like finding happiness, learning to forgive myself and others, and a commitment to walking through this life I have with love. The opposite is merely a survival tactic and a disservice to my ancestors, and to myself. It might be pressure I'm applying to myself, but I could never forgive or forget the cruelty that racism can produce and that makes me want to go harder. I feel that part of my purpose on this earth is to help heal the minds of Black people so we can continue to thrive. I aim to build enlightenment for as many Black people as possible, so we can be fully equipped to defend ourselves and offensively make sure our rights as humans are never violated in that way again. In my eyes, only playing defense against 400 years of deep-rooted oppression will forever be a losing battle.

I was in Ghana with four friends from Drexel: Ama, Giselle, Rakita, and Rashida. They'd arrived from the US a couple of days before me as I flew from Rome and planned to stay in Amsterdam for a day during a long layover. Then came the snowstorm that stranded me in the Leonardo da Vinci airport for fifteen hours due to my flight being canceled. Eventually, I was able to find a Middle East Airlines flight to Accra out of Beirut, but it was a tight timeline to get me to Beirut. The flight to Accra was scheduled to depart Beirut at the same time that I landed. When I landed in Beirut, it was only for a few minutes, but it was one of the best airport experiences I've ever had. I'd never felt so welcome. Two agents were waiting for me at the gate to escort me to my flight to Accra. They'd made sure the flight waited for me and wanted to make sure I had no problems. They even treated me with a kindness and respect at border patrol that I'd never experienced before. I told myself that one day I'd come back to experience the city in its fullness.

I hadn't spoken with my friends other than to update them on my arrival time. When I landed, they greeted me like only they can, whole tribe in tow, with the driver of the SUV we rented for the duration of our stay. We rented a house for our stay, but upon arrival, there were some issues that made it unlivable for us, so we ended up staying at the orphanage with all the kids. That had to be the highlight of the trip for me. All the kids were in such high spirits the entire time. They cared about our well-being more than I'd expected. And Ama's mom was such a gracious host. There wasn't much room for an extra group of five, but they made it work. We all slept in a single room with five mattresses on the floor, and there were no complaints. We were surrounded by love and the kids took to us immediately. They were grateful for our presence, and we were grateful for their hospitality and the opportunity to be with the kids when they woke up on Christmas morning to open their gifts. It made staying at the orphanage the best thing that could have happened to us.

Accra was full of life. Spending Christmas and New Year's in Ghana has become a world phenomenon and I feel lucky to have experienced it before the world caught on. We would go from the orphanage in Tema to mansion parties and clubs that raged all night. During the day, we explored the country and its many attractions. We spent days and some evenings at the beach. My favorite was Bojo beach. It made me fall in love with West African sunsets. There's this haze that produces a joyful glow in the atmosphere. It was like we had an extra layer of protection from the sun in the atmosphere that amplifies our melanin. I'd never experienced anything like it before and I still haven't.

I found so much love and strength in Africa during this trip to Ghana. Despite foreign occupation and the rummaging of its resources for capital gains, African culture is strong. I never realized it from the outside looking in, with only western media to look at as a source of information. But I think the world should look at Africa as a blueprint, removing the stigma of "less than." Africa has shown me that you can show love and strength simultaneously. Love does not equal weakness. We can love and make sure we don't get taken advantage of. We can love and still be strong enough to call out injustice. We can love each other and excel. I hope every African American person gets the opportunity to visit any part of Africa at least once in their lifetime. The beauty, energy, and love will positively impact lives. It surely impacted mine.

REAL WORLD

Ghana was my last trip before graduating from Drexel and entering the real world. My life has been a roller-coaster ride until this point. One in which I've experienced the highest highs as well as the lowest lows. It's given me a true understanding of just how precious and valuable life really is. I wish I had this wisdom earlier in life. All of my experiences have taught me just how extendable our capacity as humans to love, do, and be really is.

I wish I could say that after college I got a job that I loved, but it's never that easy. I ended up going into the information technology field, which was a safe career choice for me. I didn't want to tie my fate to the markets after witnessing the pitfalls of working in finance. Technology seemed like a profession where I'd always be able to get a job and it wouldn't take over my life. It was time for me to be practical, or so I thought. After all, I had lived in a bubble my entire college career. It was time to step into real life, right? The six-figure debt I graduated with was very, very real. Initially, I wanted to pursue a career as a financial advisor. I studied for six months and passed the exams for my securities license but I quickly realized the disadvantage I had in the industry. My main goal was always to serve my community. I wanted to help as many people as I could become financially stable and more aware of their options. But the wealth management field was not made for the people in my community. It was built for the wealthy to manage their wealth. The poor have no use for tax shelters, mutual funds, and investment plans when they're just trying to make ends meet.

I was pursuing this career option with ING, a financial services company. One day I walked into our Jersey City office for a big meeting with my manager and the rest of my colleagues who started at the same time as me. We'd all gathered in the big conference room for an announcement. I had no clue what was going on, but I knew it was something big. My manager walked in grinning in his three-piece suit that was tailored to perfection. He walked over to one of my colleagues who started in my class, put his hands on his shoulders, then turned to the rest of the class and said, "I want to give a huge shout-out to 'I can't remember his name' for structuring a huge enterprise insurance deal before even getting fully licensed. Here's a $60,000 commission check." Everyone around me started clapping and cheering, but I was confused. How was that even possible?

My colleague started to explain that he convinced his dad that he and his partners needed to buy large life insurance policies for each other to protect their private medical practice. I knew then that I was out of my league. I didn't get into this field for this. I wanted to help everyday people. I kept working at it, but I quickly realized that most people in my community didn't trust financial advisors because they didn't understand it—and I didn't blame them. It's purposely complicated and made for people with wealth. I decided to cut my losses and figure out some other way I could serve my community.

As the interest on my loans continued to pile up, I decided to delay a paycheck even more and accept a position at a technology consultant firm on Wall Street in which I had to participate in an unpaid technology bootcamp academy to learn about the field. The academy, which consisted of an eighteen-week curriculum over the summer taught me everything I needed to learn to begin a career in information technology. This was before companies like General Assembly and other alternative learning centers began to emerge. Comitting to this unpaid opportunity seemed like a weird thing to do given I'd just graduated college and everyone else I knew was already making money, but I wanted to give myself an edge. My gut told me that the intersection of technology and business was going to be a main driver in the future of business. I learned about operating systems and shell and database scripting, as well as technology project management. I didn't particularly enjoy it but I was good at it. I had chosen safe over purpose. I still took risks within the space, but it was small in comparison to the risks I put off that would allow me to live the life I wanted. But I was slowly beginning to finding my way.

I often think about what it means to operate in the "Real World" as a Black man. I used to believe it meant coming into adulthood and having responsibilities. For me, the real world has had more racism, vicious competition, and betrayal than I'd like to admit. Even being named after some of the country's fiercest activists, I still wasn't prepared for it. I thought by doing well I could escape it, but there's no escaping racism in America, especially as a Black man and especially as a Black man in corporate America. I can recall numerous instances when peers who were threatened by me turned against me or when I had to face their barrage of microaggressions or felt like my growth was being purposefully stifled. It all left me questioning my value. The constant attacks caused me to develop imposter syndrome.

This imposter syndrome formation was aided by the tunnel vision it took for me to get through my journey as well as the lack of purpose I felt in my jobs. It was as if suddenly I came out of the tunnel and was at my destination and I wasn't sure how I got there. While I was in the tunnel, the only thing I focused on was getting to the light; everything else was dark. Spending almost a decade going through life in that darkness made it hard for me to remember everything that was going on around me due to my low visibility, including all the work I was putting in. Being in predominantly white professional spaces, where my accomplishments didn't seem to matter because the color of my skin, made it that much worse. I had to constantly remind myself that I didn't just wake up one day to find myself in these rooms with a seat at that table. I worked for it. I belonged there, no matter how much people tried to make me feel like I didn't.

EVEN THE ODDS

I put pressure on myself to reach a level of greatness similar to the legends I'm named after, but in my own way. I had no clue what my way was, but I was determined to try as many things as I could to figure it out. With every accomplishment and accolade, I saw myself getting closer and closer to an idea of greatness without ever defining what it actually looked like for me. After graduating college and getting a job in technology at a global investment bank, I began to think about what was next. I thought to myself that this couldn't be it, the culmination of all I've fought so hard for. So, I decided to take the next step and apply to graduate school. I still had dreams of becoming an entrepreneur, I just didn't know where to begin. I figured that's what I'd go back to school to learn. If I was going to go back, this time I would set my sights on the best school for entrepreneurship, which, at that time, was the Stanford Graduate School of Business (GSB). I didn't want to get a master of business administration though. Climbing the corporate ladder wasn't the goal, and I definitely couldn't afford it.

After some research, I found an alternative. Stanford offered the Ignite program for entrepreneurship, which was the most popular program at the Business School. But did I have what it takes to be one of only thirty people accepted into the program? With only a 5 percent acceptance rate, I was sure that there were many more qualified applicants than me, but I also knew that I had a lot to offer. I had to try. The application process was an interesting journey that began toward the end of 2014, three years after I graduated from Drexel. During the process, I found that people tended to romanticize the person who gets into schools like Stanford and Harvard. They're typecast based on what they see in the media, either white or affluent Black. I didn't look the part, but I learned how to talk the talk and walk the walk. I knew that most people wouldn't want to walk a mile in my shoes, but maybe that was the key. The sacrifices and amount of work I put into graduating college and getting to this point can seem unfathomable to some, so I decided to use that to my advantage. But for the same reason, I was often met with deaf ears after mentioning that I was going to apply. No one said it, but I felt that people didn't believe I'd get in. They couldn't comprehend it. Even after all that I'd already accomplished and proved, the doubt in my abilities from others annoyed me, but it just made me go harder to prove to myself and others that it could be done. I put even more pressure on myself to do whatever it would take to get in.

There was this chip on my shoulder to constantly need to prove myself, mostly because I still saw myself as the insecure little boy from the projects in East Harlem. I knew that hundreds, if not thousands, of people from around the world would be applying and most wouldn't get accepted. I knew my odds were slim, but I also knew all I needed was a slim chance. Through it all, I had an underlying belief in myself that was as big as you can imagine because of all that I'd already accomplished. I never let my perception of the lack of encouragement from others stop me. My hustle was unstoppable. I turned into a madman on a mission, going to events, meeting as many people as possible. I had written my essays about a million times each, soliciting edits from my friends and repeatedly revising them as needed. Getting it just right so that it told my story in the context of shared values and principles of the GSB community, such as the importance of being a continual learner, which I believe I genuinely am. It's why I was so drawn to the culture at Stanford. I wanted to give myself as much of an edge as possible, so I studied everything from its mission to its student profiles extensively before even beginning to apply. Stanford was committed to looking at the totality of a student, not just grades, and the way it promoted and uplifted students affirmed my belief that it was the right school for me.

Eventually, I had to just submit my application. I had gotten to a point where I let too much noise in by soliciting opinions others and at the end of the day I had to make sure that it was my voice that reverberated throughout. My last revision was to make sure it did just that. I noticed afterward that I had made several grammatical errors, but that hadn't mattered in the end. I solicited recommendations from one of the best mentors I ever had while I was at Drexel, Chris Finnin, and my then-current executive director at Natixis, the french investment bank that I was working at. To be honest, I never thought about not getting into Stanford. It was a long shot. But I knew I had to give it my all. If I didn't get in, it wasn't going to be because of a lack of effort on my part. I was satisfied with that because I had already gotten something out of the application process: the realization of how important it was to find my voice and let it shine.

GETTING INTO STANFORD GSB

I didn't have any examples of essays that got people accepted into top schools like Stanford. I had my voice. For that reason, I wanted to share the essay prompts for the applicants and my responses. To serve as inspiration for anyone looking to pursue higher education opportunities. I feel that it's important that I don't gatekeep these things from my community so that we all have these opporunities.

1. Describe your current operational role at your organization and/or describe your current educational background and research focus.

I currently work in a small team of three as a Security Administrator for a French investment bank. As the second lead on the team I'm responsible for managing the access to 130 critical banking applications for each of the firm's 800 employees. I'm in a very fast paced, detail-oriented role. Each application is different and has intricacies that have to be closely monitored. As one of the most important roles in the firm, my team is IT savvy and has a deep understanding of how an investment bank operates. We work directly with trading sales, operations and IT teams, so we have to understand the different roles of front, middle and back office users. This makes my role very exciting as I get the chance to see all aspects of the firm while combining my interests in International Business and Technology. I jumped into the Information Technology field by enrolling in a full-time 17 week unpaid training at a Wall Street IT consultant firm after college. During my undergraduate career at Drexel University I majored in Finance, Marketing and International Business. I also minored in International Area Studies with Italian as a language. I'm passionate about working with people from other cultures and studying their patterns and behaviors. This passion inspired me to study abroad twice, once in London, then again in Rome. In my current role, most of my coworkers are French. We also have clients all over the globe who need access to our systems. We work with our clients to figure out what they need. My international experience gives me the wisdom to know how to interact with them, even with the inherent language and cultural barriers. I believe that such a global mindset can be an asset to a team in the Stanford Ignite program.

2. How do you see this program fitting into your work, career or educational Ambitions?

Experiencing the death of many family members and friends in a short period has taught me one lesson; no matter what, life goes on. But I don't fear death. My biggest fear is leaving this world without having created something that will last long after I'm gone. My work, career and educational background for the past eight years has been driven by the idea of creating something meaningful that will span decades. I've strategically tailored my education and work to gain as many skills as I could so that I can be able to formulate innovative business strategies. My business education and work in IT allows me to be able to look at concepts from multiple perspectives. I believe this can be a huge benefit to a team in the Stanford Ignite program. This program fits my ambitions because I have a passion for formulating, developing and commercializing ideas. And if admitted, whether working on a new venture or building on an existing one, I know that it will be the beginning of a legacy. Moreover, I've worked on many teams, including some new ventures, and I fully understand the importance of collaboration. That's what draws me to this program. I consider myself to be an Entrepreneur in training. Over the past few years, I've made a couple of attempts at Entrepreneurship, including being a semi-finalist in my university's' business plan competition. Now I'm ready to make a full commitment to it. I learned a lot of lessons that have helped me come up with two ideas that I would like to present. The Stanford Ignite program will help me hone in on the necessary skills to go from Entrepreneur in training to Entrepreneur.

3. What skills and perspectives do you feel you can contribute to this program?

Someone once told me to pick one thing and specialize in it. But the thought of doing one thing for the rest of my life is terrifying. I realized that the world is ever evolving and we need to be as well. A narrow focus doesn't allow for adapting and surviving in this changing world. I am driven by my hunger to have a positive impact on the world. My perspective is to always stay ahead of the curve. When I first read about disruptive technologies and innovation, I wondered how one could truly innovate if you've only ever done one thing. I believe learning is infinite and we can never really be done. I've had the opportunity to delve into a number of different fields through my undergraduate and postgraduate experiences. I've developed a broad array of skills that ignite my creativity. When I'm working on a project my inspiration draws from asking myself questions like, "how can we combine skills to produce something more efficiently?" My myriad of experiences also gives me insight into multiple target audiences. I've lived abroad and traveled the world, interacting with people from different cultures. This has provided me with an awareness of how the perception of the unknown and the different can hinder forward thinking. Once I realized how big the world was, I never looked back. I was born and raised in Spanish Harlem, but where I'm from doesn't define me, my ambition does. To me ambition is what fuels all skills. The Stanford Ignite program will help harness my ambition with my other skills to bring my vision to life. Combined with the deft skills of others in this program we can create a legacy that will help set the trajectory for how we live in this world.

THINGS COME TOGETHER

The timing of my application was perfect. For the first time in its history, Stanford GSB created a satellite campus in New York City, specifically for the Ignite program. It was the first campus in the US, other than their main one in California. It was their attempt at extending their reach to the East Coast, which meant I wouldn't have to leave my job if I was accepted.

Once I submitted my application toward the end of 2014, I let it go and freed it from my mind. I had no time to dwell on it as I was headed to South Africa to visit one of my good friends, William, and my focus immediately shifted to planning a great trip. William and I met through Ama who introduced us during our Ghana trip. We remained friends for years despite the thousands of miles between us, meeting up in cities around the world for vacations, a testament to a sincere friendship. I flew into Johannesburg in early January 2015 and was immediately struck by a feeling of belonging. The burgeoning city was reminiscent of New York City excecpt it was run by Black people. There was a large group of us that converged on the city for William's cousin's wedding. I stayed in his condo with the rest of the groomsmen. The energy was infectious, and I found myself surrounded by awesome people my entire stay. We explored the city and went on excursions while the wedding party focused on last-minute planning and rehearsals, one of which was a mini safari in Lion Park in the middle of the city.

Our driver drove us through the huge park, slowing down as we spotted a family of lions, zebras, and a host of other exotic animals for us to admire. Then, it got wild. The rules of the safari were pretty clear: when in the vehicle, you're not supposed to have your windows rolled down. We were amongst wild animals and needed a barrier for protection. But of course, we didn't follow the rules. How else were we supposed to get good pictures?

Everything was going fine until we came across a cheetah serenely lying in the shade under a large tree. The cheetah blended in with the scenery, making it almost impossible to spot. But we did. We stopped to get a good look at the animal, rolling down our windows for a better view. Almost immediately, the cheetah raised its head and quickly turned to stare at us, darting its eyes and scanning the car as if it were contemplating lunch. We quickly tried to drive away, but the car stalled. The windows wouldn't roll up and the cheetah was now standing, staring at us, trying to decide if it should pounce or not. The panic started to set in. We had all heard horror stories from this park about people getting mauled by the animals for doing the very thing we were doing. Almost instantaneously as the cheetah took a step toward us, the car started, and we were off before the cheetah could take any definitive action against us. Luck was on our side at that moment.

The energy in Johannesburg was unmatched. Our taxi driver was the real MVP. He took us everywhere we needed. I had become an occasional weed smoker and wanted to try some from the motherland. I asked our driver if he knew where I could get some, and of course, he did. He pulled up to a market on our way home from Lion Park and said, "I'll be right back." I handed him the equivalent of $10 (US), and he came back with what would be the equivalent of $100 (US) worth of weed. He had more than come through. I was the only one of the crew who smoked, so after we dropped everyone back home, we pulled up to a cul-de-sac that sat atop a hill behind the condo building where we were staying. We parked the car so that we faced the insane panoramic views of Johannesburg. The cab driver, whose name escapes me, rolled us a joint, and we started talking about our lives in between hits. I learned about his daughter and the struggles he faced trying to provide for his family, as well as high-level issues that the country and its residents were facing.

I had grown an affinity for connecting to locals in a real way when I traveled. Not just to glorify the place but to connect on a deeper level, human to human. These encounters always remind me that we are more alike than different. My time with our driver allowed me to experience Johannesburg from a working class perspective, which is what I like about traveling. With the friends I was with, we talked politics, business, and goals. With the cab driver, I had a chance to get in touch with someone who just wanted to talk about finding security to provide for his family. I could relate to both scenarios which made my experience whole. Either way though, there was a sense of calm that I had, being around people that looked like me, that I never felt when traveling to other countries. It only intensified my phlegmatic nature, maximizing the relaxation of my vacation. I never worried about racism while I was there, even though I know it still existed. It was far enough out of reach for me to not feel it in my short visit as I was surrounded by the welcoming nature of the entire wedding party. It felt like home. After our smoking session, feeling good, I let the driver keep all the weed as I just wanted a taste. And I knew it would benefit him. Culturally, sharing weed is a small gesture that means a lot to Black men. It's an offering of unity. I realized then how the feeling of gratitude and connection translates the same throughout the world amongst Black men. It creates borderless brotherhood. And I believe it's one of the reasons governments try to persecute Black men for indulging in it. They fear the power of our enlightened unity.

As soon as I got back to the US from South Africa, I received my acceptance letter to the Stanford Graduate School of Business Ignite program. The day after I landed, I was back at work, wishing I was still living it up in South Africa. I hadn't thought about Stanford at all and had forgotten that I even applied. I had no clue when I would be notified of the decision. But here I was, coming down from the high of a great trip when I received an email on my phone congratulating me on my acceptance. I must've read the email about five times to make sure I was reading it right. I was so happy, I couldn't contain myself and the smile across my face said it all. I couldn't hide my excitement. When my coworkers asked what happened, I let them know, and it was met with lackluster congratulations from some and excitement from others. At first, the lackluster congrats got to me, but I quickly let it go, realizing that I didn't care for anyone who didn't have love for me in their hearts. I just got into the best business school in the world and I was on my way. But getting in was just the first challenge. As part of my decision to apply, I convinced myself that I'd be able to get a scholarship to attend. It was the only way I could afford tuition. I told myself there was no way I'd beat the odds and get in and not be able to go due to money. I quickly applied for the scholarship right after my acceptance. A week later, I found out I was denied. Plan B. Initially when I applied, my job said it would pay for it through a tuition reimbursement benefit. But when I went to them to confirm, they denied my request. It seemed they didn't think I would get in either and were blowing smoke at me. So now I needed a new plan. I couldn't take out any more loans. I was in debt up to my neck already from undergrad. I had two weeks to figure out how I was going to get $14,500.

At the time, I was living in Brooklyn in a three-bedroom apartment with two roommates, Mike and Matt. Mike and I went through the IT academy together and both got placed at Barclays, where we worked together for a while before I moved on. He and Matt were childhood friends and were looking for a third roommate for their apartment and I decided to move in with them. After being denied the scholarship I was talking with them when I came up with the idea to do a crowdfunding campaign using the GoFundMe platform to raise the money for my tuition. At the time the platform was gaining popularity, but it wasn't as over-saturated as it is now. Setting this campaign up was one of the most uncomfortable things I've ever done. I hated asking people for money. Just the idea of asking one person for money makes me cringe, but here I was basically asking everyone I knew. My back was against the wall, and I saw no other choice. I couldn't let my fear stop me. I just decided to not think about it and move through the anxiety of the ask so fast that I didn't have time to feel how uncomfortable it made me. My cousin Shakira was my sounding board, hyping me up as I sprang into action. I knew I needed some form of visual aid that would attract attention. My roommate's dad lived in an awesome building in Tribeca, and I had the idea to do a video on the roof with the NYC skyline in the background to commemorate my hometown. That place raised me and I was now getting access to one of the top business schools in the world for the first time.

I wrote a speech, bought a selfie stick, and recorded the video on my phone, all in a day. I didn't have any time to waste. I needed to confirm my attendance with a full payment in fourteen days. Could I actually raise $14,000 in fourteen days? I wasn't sure, but I had to try. I went into a full blitz, reaching out to everyone I knew and constantly promoting on social media. I needed to bring as many people as possible into my vision. I still cringe thinking about that time. I have no problem with raising money for a cause, but this time my cause was myself; I was mad that I wasn't able to pay for it myself. To my surprise, a lot of people rallied for me. People donated what they could, promoted my cause, and sent me hundreds of encouraging words. Their words were hard to internalize because I still questioned my self-worth. At the end of the two weeks, I raised about $3,500. Even though it was a long way off from the $14,000 that I needed, it was still an impressive amount for the short window I had to fundraise. Personal fundraising was still a fairly new concept at the time, and the then dean of the GSB heard about my efforts and was extremely impressed. He had never seen anyone do that to attend the school. (Which I think speaks to the type of person that typically gets accepted into the school, but that's another issue.) When the two weeks were up, I scheduled a final call with the admissions director about the status of my fundraising and to finalize the confirmation of my participation in the program. Even though I had some success, I felt defeated going into that phone call because I knew I didn't have all the necessary funds. But to my surprise, the admissions director already had approval from the dean to make up the difference from what I had raised, no matter the amount. He was impressed not only with my fundraising efforts but with my overall application and thought I was a great addition to the cohort and did not want to lose me. It was settled. I was in. I belonged. I was ready. A new bubble emerged.

I continued working full time for the duration of the program, a program that was so intense most people quit their jobs to attend. Here I was with a demanding job, and now I was adding a demanding curriculum to my plate. I didn't have the luxury to give up my job, so I had to give up everything else. I was missing in action the entire ten weeks of the program. If it wasn't about work or school, I had no time for it. I had to put all my relationships and other obligations on hold. Too many people believed in me. I drew so many people into my vision and I couldn't let them down. I put immense pressure on myself to deliver. It was a lot, but I never once doubted my ability to excel. The program director told me the story of how he fought for me. Some of the admissions officers thought that I had done too much in college, but he made it a point to highlight the fact that all the things I did, I did in the time I was supposed to. I was given the same amount of time as everyone, but I had accomplished a lot more. It was my hustle and my relentless pursuit of greatness that would get me to the best business school in the world. My dream bubble was expanding beyond my wildest visions.

As part of the Ignite program, we not only had a full course load, but one of the main objectives was to create a business with a team. Everyone submitted a business idea, and we all voted on the top ideas we wanted to execute, narrowing from thirty-four to six, grouping us based on our preferences. I chose to work on an art startup called Artdex, as my initial idea was not selected by the class. The leader of my project was a chairman at the Museum of Modern Art. I won't go into details about the company, which is now up and running, but the time I spent with my team was equally exhilarating and exhausting. Putting six strong-minded entrepreneurs in a group to focus on one company was challenging, to say the least. We bumped heads a lot but we pulled through.

My team was very diverse: we had a billionaire entrepreneur, a head of a major TV network, marketing and pharmaceutical professionals, and me, a financial IT professional. I was the youngest on my team and the only male. (I seemed to constantly be in positions where I'm the only male. Not that I am complaining, just an observation.) But my experience was great. I was going to museum openings, having work meetings in what used to be my favorite set of buildings in New York: the set of Trump buildings that lined the Hudson River, reinventing the term "meetings with a view." But most of our team meetings would be held in the business center of the hotel where one of our team members was staying for the ten-week duration of the program. It was right across the street from the famed Plaza Hotel and after our final presentation, we had gone there to celebrate. She had a balcony the length of an entire block. It was like a scene right out of a movie. I was loving this penthouse-esque bubble I found myself in. It was a complete 180 from the rat- and roach-infested housing project I grew up in.

My experience overall was one for the books. Before Stanford, I could never fathom giving a business professor a standing ovation, especially not a professor of supply chain management. But when an entire class of leaders and visionaries stands up after a lecture to applaud the professor, you get it. The ability to make learning fun, interesting, and engaging is what makes Stanford the best. When you're surrounded by the best of the best, the energy is electrifying, even if only for a short period of time. It changes you. It changed my perception of what's possible within human capacity. More importantly though, I felt comfortable being myself in a space that was reserved for the best with people from all over the globe and different walks of life who came together for a judgment-free but competitive experience that allowed everyone to bring out their best. The competition sometimes brought out our worst; it wasn't easy having to figure out how to work together with individuals who were all experienced, strong leaders. But that was the beauty of it. Learning how to manage the strongest personalities to come together for a common goal taught me valuable lessons about how to pick my battles. I had to quickly learn when to hold on to my convictions regarding certain topics and when to compromise for the greater good of progress. It was a more intense experience than similar ones in undergrad because we were playing on a higher level with experienced and opinionated professionals who all had a real stake in the outcome. I no longer had an interest in being a leader amongst the blind. It's easy to lead the visionless.

Stanford GSB's motto is: "Change lives. Change organizations. Change the world." Little did I know that changing myself would be just as massive an undertaking as any of those other attributes. I wanted to change the world but had no clue what I wanted as an outcome. What I've realized is that wanting to change the world is more than a sound bite. For the most successful, there's a how and why behind their ambition that drives them. What was driving mine? Being surrounded by so many purpose-driven individuals deafeningly exposed my shortcomings. I had only cracked the surface of my voice.

CORPORATE POLITICS AS USUAL

One of the things I never learned in college or as a junior-level employee in corporate America is that once you reach a certain point in your career, you'll need to become a politician. That's what a seat at the table means. You become a political representative, and as a person of color with a seat at the table, it often comes with expectations of you "playing ball." As soon as you begin to form your own opinion, and the "leaders" realize they can't control you, you'll no longer serve a purpose to them. Coporate America can be cutthroat. And I'd always been competitive, but it's always been me vs me. I've always been about letting my work shine through. But as Black man in corporate america shining brought on the haters. The people who saw my light and skills and wanted nothing more that to tear me down because they feared my potential. People fear the unknown, especially when it illuminates their weaknesses. I never felt the need to lie or manipulate to bring somcone else down to make myself look better, so it caught me off guard when I realized this is the game I signed up for. The political dysfunction within some of the organizations I've worked for never allowed too much space for me to excel. I had to kick in the doors and demand my worth. But I made sure that I had an undeniable track record with me. Because the status quo that enables the intended organizational dysfunction will never change if we don't push for it. The unknown is scary, do it scared.

Preservation of self often became the goal over diversity, equity, and inclusion (DEI) of thought and/or actions whenever I dared to challenge the status quo. I knew that this mindset, if not checked, could lead to the downfall of an organization. But the power to make actual change has to come from the will of the leadership. DEI is a complex topic because the systems in which its meant to affect are rooted in deep-seated oppression that tells its members in order to be successful in our system this oppression must be upheld. This is why I believe that any credible discussion regarding DEI should not run from its complexity but toward it. Real change is made by facing the hard stuff. This sentiment is echoed throughout every industry that utilizes any form of technology. Technology changes rapidly, and my experience in the field has taught me that the preservation of outdated, legacy tech systems is a strategy rooted in preservation of self over advancing an organization. With new tech comes new skills, which can lead to many individuals becoming superfluous if they don't adapt. In this way, technology mirrors the outdated, legacy systems of racism and oppression in America. American culture in its purest form is anti-progress.

Racial discrimination in the workplace is just as prevalent today as ever, but the constant gaslighting has caused speaking up about it to be considered taboo, to say the least. In 2016, I was working at Natixis, a french investment bank, when I was promoted to manage a vital technology department. I was twenty-seven years old, and it was a big deal for me as a young Black man in this highly visible role. I felt like things were coming together for me. I saw myself on an upward trajectory. But after months of stalling from Human Resources, I was told that I had to work for an additional year before getting the pay raise that went along with the promotion. At this point, I was in a vice president position with an analyst pay grade. After trying to understand why, I was told by the global head of Human Resources that they thought I'd just be happy I was in the position, as if I were a freed slave given the opportunity to lead the house. I felt like my offer letter was Field Order No. 15, promising me "forty acres and a mule." This man who boldly disrespected me to my face wasn't Andrew Johnson, but the revocation of what was promised to me felt reminiscent of his reversal of Field Order No. 15.

I'd gotten the opportunity because I was the most qualified to do the job, yet I spent months not getting a straight answer from anyone about my pay. I was constantly stymied by the cancellation of meetings and refusals to give me a direct answer; this caused me to be more strident in my vocalization of how I felt about the entire situation. There was a lot of posturing that felt like a preamble to something, but I didn't know what. I needed to find out, which is why I pressed every executive I could about it. I felt like I couldn't let them play me like this. My ancestors worked for free for too long and I refused to follow the same fate. Experience is not an acceptable form of payment to me. Contrary to popular belief, Black people are not happy to work for experience. The premise is racist and insulting at best, and I expressed that to the HR director after he suggested it. The day after my meeting with the head of HR, I was laid off.

In this same position, before I was let go, it was my job to hire an analyst to expand my team. After putting out the job description, the mostly white HR team sent me a list of qualified candidates, but I couldn't believe the lack of quality candidates I was receiving. It got to a point where I ended up burning a bridge with a colleague who wanted me to hire his extremely inept son for the sensitive position in which I was hiring, a position that was directly responsible for all the firm's operations. His son didn't even bother to come presentably to the interview, as if it was just a formality. A suit was the typical interview attire, and he strolled into the office as if he'd just rolled out of bed. I was floored by the audacity of his perceived privilege. I didn't hire my colleague's son, and that was the end of our relationship.

The stakes were too high for nepotism. I couldn't fail in this position. There were too many eyes on me, the twenty-seven-year-old Black man who essentially had the "keys to the kingdom." After an underwhelming round of interviews, I requested that HR send me all the resumes they received for the position, not just the ones they deemed acceptable. I went through them in my free time and took them home to review as well. To my surprise, there were many great candidates that never made it to me, candidates with names more commonly associated with Black individuals. I didn't say anything about this but I did request interviews for the candidates I liked, making a point to bring in the qualified Black candidates.

My lessons from going against the grain, taking charge, and not just accepting what someone puts in front of me prepared me for that moment, and I finally found the candidate that I wanted to hire. He was more qualified than all the others and he just happened to be a young Black man as well. HR tried everything but flat-out telling me no to get me not to hire him. They even offered up a candidate who wasn't nearly as qualified but who was a white woman. After rejecting this candidate whom they tried to force on me, I was then forced into meetings with my executive director and HR to defend my choice, which I did, unemotionally. I never brought up the obvious, but I was annoyed at the hoops I had to go through to hire another Black man. They really hated to see it but, in the end, they couldn't deny my defense and I got the candidate I wanted for the job. Neither one of us lasted long, but I made sure we got the most out of the opportunity. I heard the extremely unqualified white woman whom I didn't hire got hired after I was out.

To get hired at a company like that when you're a Black man, there has to be a decision maker who will advocate for you. Being qualified isn't enough. We can't be afraid to advocate for each other, especially when racism is embedded in business as usual. Making that decision to hire another Black man was easy. Getting buy in from others was the difficult part. I never imagined it would be as difficult as it was, especially when it was my decision to make. But I stood my ground. Because at the end of the day, I knew that we belonged.

When you're young, Black, and gifted, never doubt whether people recognize your potential. They do. Your potential is your power and there will be some who'll try and block you from reaching that potential. This is especially true when they're aware that you can do things they cannot. They won't acknowledge it, and they'll think it's their job to humble you. See through it and never waiver in your quest to reach your highest potential. Paying it forward as you ascend.

Right after I was laid off from Natixis, I quietly left the building with my head held high. I knew it was their loss, and I knew that I did everything in my power to advocate for what I deserved. But there was a sting that still haunts me. It was the first time I'd ever been escorted out of a building. The abruptness and finality cut me deep. I'd given my all to that job, and here I was being tossed aside like I never mattered. I called my father to let him know what happened. He was with my uncle and they both assured me that everything will be OK. After I hung up, I went to the gym. The Equinox in Rockefeller Center was my sanctuary where I could go after a day of dealing with the stress that came with the job. It was a gym and a spa all in one. It's what I think of when I think about the perks of living in New York City—that and the food. After the gym, I wanted to treat myself, so I went to Phillipe Chow for lunch, ordered a Scotch, and reminded myself of my greatness. It was my way of not letting them tear down my self-worth.

One of the hardest things for me to let go of was the fact that as a Black man in America, I'd often be in situations where I'd have no control over my life the way others did. That my life could be taken away from me by a system put in place with that specific purpose. It's a feeling that you can't truly comprehend unless you're a Black man. There's real danger for us around every corner and it's rooted in prejudice and bias. We're seen as threats to so many, the worst of it being from individuals who hide behind their indifference, so they don't have to recognize their own bias, and they never have to face their actions with a prejudicial lens. We're fighting battles at work, at school, and every day in a world that refuses to accept our greatness. The only thing that matters is that we accept our greatness.

I've had two corporate positions since that role at Natixis before taking a much-needed two-year break. In my last corporate position, I worked at a financial technology company called Hedgeserv; they managed the reporting and administrative tasks for hedge funds with about $350 billion in assets under administration. I recognized early on how little value my input had, so I decided I would fall back on climbing this particular ladder there and focus on being more observant.

I used it as an educational experience in people and politics. I didn't have the energy, or pay grade to try and fit into their culture. But it was the environment I chose to work in. I needed to get the technical experience to learn the ins and outs of the industry as well as emerging technologies and that's what they offered . One of the biggest lessons that I've learned and hope to bring to my own organization is that work should be a meaningful aspect of one's life. Work culture should be a safe space where everyone comes together for a collective mission, whatever that mission may be. Everyone's input, no matter how small or large, should be a vital part of the ecosystem that keeps the mission alive. Employees should feel as though their contribution is important and the leadership's job is to be vocal about this and pull their employees into the company mission, not just with empty words or rebranding attempts but with every decision that's made.

I usually tried to keep to myself regarding certain topics in the workplace. But sometimes, I got drawn in. I've experienced many incidents of racism over my career, but there are a couple that stand out for being very overt. In some corporate cultures, the axiomatic air of racism and harassment fills the room. Employees are expected to not only sit back and accept the way things are but to participate as well or have their careers stifled after being left on the outside. If keeping my integrity and character intact means sacrificing being a part of a club, then I'll ecstatically demur on my way out. What I've learned is that people want you to engage them. It makes them feel powerful, superior even, if they think they know your triggers. I've encountered a lot of people in corporate america who loved trying to race-bait with me just to turn around and act like they were the victim of the encounter. They couldn't figure me out so this was their way to trigger an emotional response from me. I was constantly tested to with the aim of trying to find my triggers, so they can know what to use against me when they needed to. I've learned that having the strength to recognize and not engage was the biggest display of power I could make. The power over myself. Because as soon as you engage, you show your cards, and you hand your power over to the other person. And they'll pull that trigger when and where they want, whether it's to get what they want or just because they can.

I'd endured a lot of harassment and racism during my tenure at Hedgeserv which made it feet like I was living in a matrix. Every day there were new attempts at gaslighting me. I knew I'd had enough when my director told me to remind him to never go to a Starbucks with me, after he questioned other white colleagues about whether the 2018 incident in Philadelphia, when two black men were arrested for sitting in Starbucks, was racist or not. I never allowed them to evoke any emotion from me with these kinds of statements but suddenly I found myself being removed from high-visibility projects where I was set to lead, and I wondered if it was because they realized they couldn't affect me in the way that probably worked for them before on other Black men they tried to control. Their narrative of me touted expressions reminiscent of the typical microaggressions like, "I'm not a team player" or "I lacked enthusiasm," etc. But what do you expect from someone you constantly harass?

After a year it'd become an extremely hostile and toxic work environment for me, and I no longer cared to engage. It never affected my actual work though. In fact, my productivity increased, although they told me that I wasn't producing enough. Everything that I went through made me think about what it was I was working so hard for, other than the obvious paycheck. When Raylin died, I had to keep going because I was fighting for myself. I was still in school and I needed a bachelor's degree more than anything to kickstart my career. It was a tangible thing, with specific steps on what to do to attain it. But then, while I was at Hedgeserv, I experienced a tragedy like no other, and was met with little to no compassion. Here I was, killing myself for a company that didn't give a fuck about me. It didn't seem right. I deserved better. If I was going to put on my gloves again fight for my life, I knew I had to find something more meaningful. I thought to myself, if I must work for an organization I don't own, I'm going to make sure that I choose one with a mission that's aligned with mine. Company culture, executive leadership, and dedication to employees became my new barometer. I first had to figure out what my personal mission was, so I crafted the following statement.

Personal Mission: *My mission is to live in light as someone who's once lived in the dark. I want to be an example for others who may need a guide. I want to take on my responsibility as a human to help positively advance humanity in any way that I can. To speak up when necessary on issues that are immoral, unethical, or inhumane. And to be a leader in all my pursuits who always puts people before profits.*

WHEN THE UNTHINKABLE HAPPENS AGAIN

I had been in therapy for a few months when I started to feel happy again and like my old self. I initially wanted to go because I was feeling stuck in all areas of my life. It was a very difficult decision for me. I didn't know anyone else who was in therapy. Especially no other Black men. I kept it a secret for a while. Like it was something to be ashamed of. I knew my family wouldn't be supportive. When I finally opened up to my parents about it, they didn't understand why I felt the need to go to therapy. Especially my dad who just dismissed the idea altogether. But despite the judgment and lack of support, I knew it was something I needed to do for myself. And I never shied away from doing whatever I needed to for my growth. At the time I didn't feel much sense of purpose. My career felt like it was stalling, constantly being undermined in racist and toxic work environments. I needed help sorting out what internally was keeping me blocked and how to deal with it. Working with my therapist helped me put a lot in perspective and helped me confront my grief and my fears. The most important thing that I learned in therapy was how to ask myself the hard questions. And how to process my answers. And it was working. I was beginning to see the light at the end of the tunnel again. I moved into in a new apartment in Harlem and, while my job at Hedgeserv was challenging, I focused on the things I could gain while there.

My thirtieth birthday was approaching and I decided that I wanted to plan a big party to bring together all my loved ones and afterward set off on a trip to Japan. I had a lot to celebrate. I'd never had all my friends and family from all the different areas of my life together at once. I thought it would be really special to make that happen for my thirtieth. About two weeks before the big day I decided to go out for drinks with my friend Robert after work, who was also my coworker and one of the coolest guys I'd ever worked with. It was the first time in a few months I'd done that, as I was focused on improving my mental health. At this point, I was happy, not feeling stuck, and at a point where I was ready to move forward fast again. After some bar hopping I got home around 1:00 a.m., slightly inebriated. I laid down in bed without a care in the world, and then my phone started to ring. I didn't recognize the number, but it was a Winter Park, Florida, area code. I knew Winter Park from the times I visited Coco, so I picked up. It didn't matter what time it was, I always picked up for Coco. Whatever she needed, I'd be there for her. That's just how we were. We'd survived a lot together and knew we'd always be there for each other no matter what. She was only 1 year older than me and had just turned 31. We were more like siblings than cousins.

When I first saw the number I thought maybe Coco got a new number and wanted to talk. But when I picked up, on the other line was her boyfriend, Jamie. He was crying and I could barely make out what he was saying. And then it hit me like a ton of bricks: Coco was dead. I could only make out a few words between his sobs and I had to say those words back to him to make sure I understood him correctly. "Are you telling me that my cousin is dead?" "Yes," he replied.

I couldn't quite wrap my head around what was happening and I couldn't think straight, so I hung up the phone. I slapped myself a couple of times to make sure I was awake and not some king of drunken dream state. I called Jamie back after a few minutes once I sobered up a bit. I needed him to clarify, to make sure this wasn't some sick joke. It wasn't. He explained how the police had just left their apartment to notify him of her passing. She was in a car accident in which she was thrown out of the back seat and died instantly. At that moment, so did I. My heart stopped when I realized what was happening and then it shattered into a million pieces. He went on to let me know that because she was working so much and was too tired to drive, she left her car in the parking lot of her office building and opted to carpool with coworkers instead. The driver who survived the crash, collided with another car that was speeding and lost control. It was at this point that I realized that I was the only one in my family to know that she was gone, so I couldn't collapse as much as I wanted to. I felt the enormity of the responsibility of what had to happen next. I had to muster enough strength to break the news to everyone, a conversation I'd go on to have multiple times that night. Every conversation broke my heart into a million more pieces. First with my mom, then my dad, my brother, and my aunt and uncle. I labored over how to do it, but, in the end, there was no easy way. It's a feeling that I don't wish on anyone; after that job was done, I had no more strength.

When I think about how it all transpired I'm often left with the idea that if she'd just put on her seat belt, she might be alive today. To have the wherewithall to not drive because she was too tired, but not put on a seat belt is somethign I wrestle with. Because even when we think we're making the right decision, it can go terribly wrong. But a lesson that I've learned from this is that no matter what, everytime I get in a moving vehicle I'll always put on my seatbelt. And I hope that her story can be impactful to others and motivate them to always wear a seat belt as well. It doesn't matter if you're the driver, the passenger, or in the back seat. Your seat belt could be the only thing between life or death. Life is short enough, don't give it any shortcuts. Honestly, I try and find the silver lining in all this, but it was very difficult for me to accept that she was gone. She had so much to offer this world.

RETURNED TO SENDER: LETTERS TO SOULS IN THE HEREAFTER

Dear Coco,

The brightest star in my universe. Never could I have imagined our lives would come to this. I don't think I'll ever understand why this happened to you. In my grief, I try to remember that this happened to you and not me, but it makes it worse because I wish it was the other way around. But at least you're spared this pain. When the reality of your passing gets too heavy for me, I have plenty of awesome memories of you that instantly light me up. Your passion for music rubbed off on me so much, and I'm so grateful for that. Music has always helped guide me. I remember growing up how we would often stay up listening to music, mostly hip-hop, writing the lyrics down so we could memorize them, then rapping along with the artist. Back when cassette tapes were a thing, before CDs that included the lyrics in the packaging, before Google. We had so much fun dissecting music and creating our own. All those quintessential black-and-white notebooks filled with raps about life were the archetype of our dreams. And the fact that you never gave up on yours, dedicating your life to music and helping to uplift underground artists, giving them a platform to be heard is so admirable. I admired you.

I'm so proud of what you accomplished, and I know you know that already, but I'd shout it from the rooftops any chance

I get. The insurmountable odds you overcame deserve adulation. The strength you had at such a young age to know something was wrong at home, leave, and hop on a train to travel to Harlem by yourself showed just how smart and capable you were. And you never let up, nor did you ever let not having your father or mother in your life make you jaded. We were your family and we were enough. Your smile was infectious. You had a personality that lit up any room you entered. I think that's why your death hit so hard for all of us. You were truly one of a kind and everyone who knew you lost the privilege of your essence, a void that could never be replaced.

I'm so thankful that I started going to therapy before you passed. It really helped me push through this. After Raylin died, we were all going through it in our own ways. But the way you picked yourself up and changed your life was so inspiring to me. Deciding to chase your dreams of working in the music and entertainment business, after facing what has seemed like all the adversity in the world, was no easy feat. But you went on to graduate with a bachelor's and a master's degree in entertainment business from Full Sail University, a school that's known for producing award-winning artists, producers, etc. I just knew you were going to be next on its list of accomplished alumni. When you started your own artist management company, I felt like you were beginning to come into your own. And working full time while doing it? Your grind was insane. You were living out your dream in the pursuit of your happiness. It kills me that your life was cut short and so tragically. But as difficult as it is, I try not to question your destiny. I just hope that you're at peace. Because you deserve it. I'll miss you forever. Love Always, Queen, - Your Biggest Cheerleader

WILDFIRE

I survived for a long time by going against the grain. Doing what I thought was right for me, instead of succumbing to the status quo and emulating the lifestyle of the environment I was in. I never used drugs, when everyone around me was using. I stood against violence, even when it seemed like the only way to survive. Even deciding to take on debt and go to college when no one else in my family had ever been. Trusting myself and my vision for my life was difficult. But It led to many successes and grew my confidence over time. But even that trust and confidence couldn't prepare me for the price I'd have to pay for success. In both monetary and non-monetary ways. I understood that you need money to make money, and my definition of success was making money. It's why I never hesitated when it came to taking out student loans or maxing out my credit card on books and living expenses. It's the price I was paying for my eventual success. But what life has shown me about success is that the price it demands is far greater than any monetary value: it's time. And, unfortunately, I didn't realize this until it was too late. For me, payment was due in the form of lost time with my loved ones before they passed. It's a price I keep paying in pursuit of a dream that may never come to fruition and that realization confused me to a point of destruction. I'd convinced myself that I would be successful. Failure wasn't an option. But the pain of missing out on precious time with my loved ones had me wondering if it was worth it. I was forced to question everything I thought I knew to be true about my priorities and how I should move in this world, thinking I had to be closed off to succeed. Loss made me question what success really meant for me.

For so long, my picture of success was based on superficial societal beliefs of greatness, embracing the hunger for more as if there was a great wildfire inside me ferociously seeking more forests to set ablaze. Like a wildfire, my sole intention was to shine brightly, vigorously push through obstacles, and unapologetically expand my reach. I needed to reach as much as I could as fast as I could. I never stopped to get a bird's-eye view to see if I was leaving any destruction in my wake. All I could do was burn. It wasn't until my fire was put out by Coco's passing, that I was able to get a true measure of the wreckage I'd caused and try to investigate how I got here. From my relationships with the people I love, to my mental, physical, and financial health. This books serves as that investigation and becoming self aware. And during my journey of internal and external investigating something amazing happened. I realized I get to rebuild.

But even the thought of rebuilding myself with this new-found wisdom felt like an insurmountable undertaking, especially when thinking about the time I'd never get back. It made the idea of becoming whole and well feel like a betrayal to myself and my loved ones because I needed to tap into the same intensity to rebuild that caused the damage in the first place. Which meant more isolation. But when I reached rock bottom after Coco passed, I had no choice. I felt like I had nowhere else to go but up. I started by planting one seed. Day by day, I pushed through my anxiety and my feelings of being immensely over-whelmed, just so I could survive the day. Even though the wild-fire brought destruction, it also brought opportunity. This time, I'd have to figure out a framework to find balance and limit destructive behavior.

Patience was the key I couldn't find until I started to let go of the idea that I could still burn the way I used to with the little bit of spark I had left. I had to mentally let go of the weight of all my responsibilities, except for one, getting better. I couldn't bear the weight of the image I'd created for myself as a pillar of strength, my abilities at work, or worry-ing about others. I thought there was dishonor in that, even though I knew I would come back for it when I was ready. I passed the time between days by using whatever spark I had to get stronger and create more fire. But there were a lot of dark, fireless days, and with those days came an element of peace that caused me to fear the fire. I figured if I could muster enough courage to study how to properly manage my fire, I could create a balance that could bring me happiness. Because happiness was the key that would allow peace and fire to live harmoniously within.

"If you stick a knife in my back nine inches and pull it out six inches, there's no progress. If you pull it all the way out that's not progress. Progress is healing the wound that the blow made. And they haven't even pulled the knife out much less heal the wound. They won't even admit the knife is there."

\- Malcolm X

PART 2:

HEAL, BY ANY MEANS NECESSARY

MONEY IS TRAUMATIC

Coming to grips with just how short and unfair life can be put so much in perspective for me. I hope that when I leave this earth in the physical form, everyone I've left behind can talk about the impact I had on their lives and the value our relationship brought them. I'm so happy to have had relationships with Raylin, Coco, my grandparents, Steve, and all my other family and friends who have passed on. They are my guides/compasses/North Stars to Love, Loyalty, Happiness, Positivity, and Strength. This is the story I've only recently begun telling myself after creating a framework for accepting loss.

This framework helped me work out my internal struggle about how I choose to accept the things that I cannot change. I often thought about the white man who decided to take justice into his own hands and shoot Raylin in the back, even though he was unarmed. I often thought about the reckless driver whose split-second decision cost Coco her life. I often thought about the medical staff whose negligence led to my grandfather's death. But I don't think about them very often anymore. When I used to think about these things, I'd find myself going down a rabbit hole of vengeance and of finding these men and using whatever power that I could muster to inflict on them the same kind of pain I felt. But I knew if I focused my energy on revenge, it would consume me and I wouldn't be able to heal. Besides, the revenge rabbit hole I often found myself going down, giving my mind unencumbered access to all possibilities, never ended honorably. Those individuals who held some responsibility for the deaths of my loved ones held no significant impact on the life they lived while they were here. I knew I wanted to honor that somehow. I couldn't let their death define their lives. I had to reframe the story so that I could figure out how to honor their lives in a way only I could. That was much more important to me. So, I decided to deny myself vengeance. I still can't find forgiveness in my heart. With purposeful forgetting I could deny them any more of my mental capacity which seemed like a much better way for me to move on. I forgive myself for not being able to forgive them though.

I needed to figure out what justice could look like that was acceptable to me. By immortalizing all my loved ones I've lost with my words and actions on their behalf, I knew that how I show up in the world will also be a direct reflection of them. But I didn't know if that was enough. I thought a lot about the underlying reason for their deaths while trying to figure out what more I could do. I had to dig deeper to get beyond the surface-level reasons. I realized that poverty or the lack of money and resources played a large role. A root that sprouted branches of decisions and actions that would eventually lead to their demise. I figured that by helping Black people out of poverty, myself included, I could contribute somehow to our survival. The average wealth for Black people was at $3,557 in 2016 and is estimated to decrease to $0 by year 2053. The average wealth for White people was $146,984 in 2016 and is estimated to continue to increase. This is based on a study published by the Institute of Policy Studies regarding racial wealth trends. Poverty is one of the biggest threats to our livelihood. Charles Darwin said only the strong survive, but today, only the wealthy survive. Natural selection will be defined by the wealthiest individuals who'll have the resources to not only define what evolution looks like but also who gets access and an opportunity to evolve. I once thought education and a job were the best ways to get out of poverty. I still think they are great catalysts, but that can't be the end game.

Working in corporate america while trying to heal was a challenge for me because I always had to be on. The expectations of bringing 100 percent every day seemed rooted in the same stereotypes that suggest Black men and women are immune to pain and thus should be able to do and be more than others. I guess for a while I believed that myself. I pushed myself to prove that to be true. It wasn't until I experienced a pain so heavy that I couldn't bring 100 percent of myself to work on a daily basis. That was when the microaggressions and gaslighting got worse, like being told that I wasn't pulling my weight (even though I'd be doing more than most on my bad days). They placed certain expectations on me and, if I couldn't deliver, the first instinct wasn't to help me get better but to put me down and showcase disappointment for not rising to their expectations. I was doing the same thing to myself, but to be honest, in order to get hired, I had to be the best. It's unfair, but it's the reality of the society in which we live when most see you as a threat. To what? I have no clue. I also noticed that owning the responsibility of making others around me feel comfortable in my presence was part of those expectations. It was exhausting. But after Coco died, I stopped caring about how others see me, especially in the workplace. I decided I was going to show up as my full self and not care about making others feel comfortable. In some sense, I felt a responsibility to not dim who I was because Coco no longer had a choice, but I did. I also hated the idea of being a token Black guy expected to conform so that the powers that be know they could control me. That's where their comfortableness lay. "Can I control this Black man?" No, you cannot!

The angry Black person stereotype is one of the most annoying as it's rooted in guilt. Because if someone did to them, what they do to us, they'd be angry. Their fear is just projection. I've noticed that most of the leaders I've come across who uses fear as a tactic often use it to feal secure within themselves. Their manipulation is all they have. That's why I believe everyone needs to go on a healing journey. To me feeling secure within oneself first and foremost is the foundation for effective leadership. Once I was able to spot this in other people I knew I would rather be feared and in control of myself than let someone think that their scare tactics can move me. So, I decided to constantly praise myself so that I'd never need to rely on praise from others, especially if I was to continue being in majority white spaces. Praise is always welcome but never needed, and I started using affirmations to help shift my mindset.

It wasn't an easy journey for me though. Trying to heal in a work environment that lacked compassion for its employees was disheartening, to say the least. I often had to fight hard just to get out of bed and show up to work every day. Not because I didn't like my job, although I didn't, but because of the internal turmoil I was facing after losing Coco. I had to try to be my normal self because that's what was expected of me, even though I was clearly not OK. I couldn't be human for a while without my job being in jeopardy. They discarded their employees as soon as it fit them. And during my small window of time, during which I had no fight left in me, I found myself next on the chopping block. And for a lot of Black people in coporate america who have student loans, and take care of their family and extended families, the loss of a paycheck can be devastating. We shouldn't have to live one paycheck away from financial ruin. That added stress is unhealthy. And that is the goal of white supremacy.

Racist acts aren't only the ones that involve a grand gesture that overtly showcases bias. It's the individuals who are the most offended by the idea of being called racist that you need to look out for. Their lack of will to understand and become aware usually causes their bias to subtly be projected onto their everyday actions without them consciously realizing it, actions like creating laws, policies, hiring decisions, algorithms, etc. But to this day, even in the face of american racism, we prevail so that we can get a check, which is a beautiful thing. Get your money, Black people! My advice: just don't compromise yourself getting it. That's what I felt like I was doing. So I had to make the decision to make myself a priority. I stuck with my job that I hated after Coco died but I tapped into my coping mechanisms hard, which included overworking and constantly moving and traveling to keep myself busy so that I wouldn't have any room to let in my grief. I began using all my energy to focus on healing through movement and didn't have any left to fight with my coworkers or look for another, more employee-centric job. I planned a bunch of international and domestic trips and I needed my paychecks to fund this part of my healing process. And so I embarked on this year of movement with every intention to finish stronger.

YEAR OF MOVEMENT

Never in a million years would I have imagined being a person that wanted to give up on life. But after Coco died, here I was at thirty years old, the fire within smothered by grief. I was depressed and thinking about giving up on all that I worked for. The caprices of my mental health were worsening as I insisted on suffering in silence. No one knew. No one could tell. I became deft at hiding my feelings from myself and others. I started to ask myself questions like: How did I get here? How do I get the pain to stop? I felt like I was drowning and I desperately wanted to come up for air. So, I decided to attack my healing the same way I attacked my other goals. I committed 100 percent, and it became the only thing that mattered to me. I had to save myself. It was a long, painful, lonely process, and I'm a completely different person today than I was before I started this journey.

The relationship I have with myself had to become my most important relationship. I found love and value for myself in ways I'd never expereinced. It made me realize a couple of things. First, I didn't know who I was wholly as an individual. I was always moving at a fast pace, so I never took the time to reflect and officially establish who Stevland Martin Malcolm Polite is as a person. The first half of my life, I often defined myself as Raylin and Coco's cousin. I always looked to them for guidance. I'm such an independent person now, but I had to grow into that, especially during the second half of my life when I was thrown into a system no one close to me knew about.

Being a first-generation college student forced me to lean into my independence as a means of survival. I knew that to succeed I couldn't count on anyone else but me. I sought to learn as much as I could about the system I was thrown into, but this independence led to conflicting narratives that caused some of my internal struggle. The disconnect was between self-reliance and self-love. I always thought they were one and the same, but I've found the difference to be staggering. This healing journey has taught me that I never really knew what love was because I never loved myself unconditionally. I often did whatever I needed to survive and not so much of anything for love.

When I decided to travel the world, it became my truest and most consistent love. As a kid, I had plenty of love around me, but growing up in a tough environment such as East Harlem, where survival was always first and foremost, love always seemed conditional. When it wasn't, I could barely recognize it. Or, at the very least, I didn't know how to actively acknowledge it. Men don't talk about things like love enough, especially with each other. We tend to show it in our actions. But sometimes we can't meet the expectations of a loved one, which can cause feelings of failure to creep in and create issues of self-worth. I never had a framework for self-love, so every time I failed to meet a condition of a loved one, it created trauma. Unpacking those things and understanding that my value and worth was not dependent on meeting others conditions helped me release those traumas.

That trauma seemed to constantly happen to me, especially

when I felt as though I failed to be the person my father wanted me to be. This pattern often caused me to retreat into self-deprecating habits such as substance use; I was creating a vicious cycle of love and hate. I realize now how those habits subconsciously affected me. I had a love/hate relationship with myself that added to my depression whenever I felt like I failed to meet a condition I placed on myself. These conditions were unhealthily disguised as ambition, which led to developing a bad habit of replacing failed conditions with new ones, as well as an addiction to the feeling of accomplishment whenever I did meet my conditions. This chase created more ambitious conditions which often required a lengthy time frame to accomplish. But patience always seemed like a virtue my survival couldn't afford.

This cycle is how problems arose from the in-between times, when the feeling of accomplishment from comparatively smaller goals no longer satisfied me. I craved the big wins so much that day-to-day life became mundane. It caused a declaration of war against myself when I could no longer escape my mind or hide behind my work. I faked it till I made it, to a certain degree at least, and then I couldn't fake it anymore. I often used sex and alcohol as a filler, anything to avoid what I was hiding from. I experimented as much as possible and got close to the edge of destruction just so I could feel something. I got to a point where I couldn't see the light at the end of the tunnel anymore. I searched for a new condition I could work toward, but nothing made sense. I was stuck in the darkness and, since I couldn't see forward, a state that was completely new to me; I had no choice but to be more mindful of my present. I needed to live in the moment, as they say, but I couldn't do that until I looked back and got a true understanding of how I got to my then-present state.

Self awareness didn't come easy. My mind was at direct odds with my personality, which fueled my curiosity and thirst for knowledge, the heartbeat of my dreams. The more my mind fought to hide things from me, the more my curiosity wanted to find them. My curiosity typically won all the external battles it went up against, but my mind was its most formidable opponent equipped with its own fortress. It was a long war. My mind won most battles, but it wasn't until I started this healing journey that curiosity began to win this mental civil war. I had begun acquiring the tools that were strong enough to break down the fortress. Suddenly, I no longer felt the need to run from my mind and the fear of the fire subsided after I learned to embrace my true feelings by facing my trauma.

When I realized that Coco was gone, I felt the fire within leave my body in a physical exchange of energy. My fire was replaced with sorrow and sadness and the light I relied on for guidance was being held hostage by darkness. To get it back, I leaned on the little spark I could muster, trying to push through and continue living life to the fullest. I placed another condition on myself which sparked my year of movement, which I was fortunate enough to have the income to see through. I went on six trips in one year, more than any other year of my life. The first was a solo trip to Japan that I took only three weeks after Coco's funeral. It was a gift to myself for my thirtieth birthday. I started planning the trip before Coco passed. I booked my flight after I snagged a flight deal earlier in the year. I thought about canceling after her funeral as nothing else was planned, but I couldn't. I had talked to Coco a couple of weeks before she passed about the trip and, although she thought I was crazy for going alone, she was supportive of my dreams to see the world. So, I decided to go and not hold back. I splurged on great hotels and did everything I wanted to do. "Say Yes" was the name of the game I was playing.

Visiting Japan was my first intercountry solo trip, and it was a big one. Thinking about what I really wanted to do and not having to worry about anyone else felt like freedom. That was what my year of movement was about, showing up to new environments as my whole self. I needed a reprieve from the familiar, where my pain seemed the heaviest, as I was no longer able to support the masks I wore to survive. I needed to continue to practice adapting to new situations without those masks. At the time, it felt like the only way I could learn how to adapt to the reality of this new life without Coco. The movement was necessary for my survival.

I traveled to three different cities in Japan. As soon as I landed in Osaka, I was immediately met with some adversity: my luggage never made my connecting flight. Here I was in a foreign land with nothing but my carry-on and backpack and with nothing but the clothes on my back. I spent the first couple of days being a typical tourist and took in the beauty of the Japanese cherry blossom season. New life was sprouting up all around me. The tone of the trip was set. I'd find myself in multiple situations where my plans were thwarted and I'd have to let go of what I couldn't control and embrace the adventurous nature of the trip. The first thing I did on this trip was visit Osaka Castle, where I dressed up as a traditional Japanese Samurai, channeling my inner warrior. Osaka started the trip and offered the most laid-back experience of all three cities. I didn't do much besides walk around and eat. I was the most adventurous with food in Osaka, but Kyoto and Tokyo offered their own unique adventures.

After Osaka, I traveled to Kyoto, where I visited a bunch of temples; one, in particular, left a priceless impression on me and my family that's still affecting us today. The Kinkaku-ji Temple, aka the Golden Pavilion, is said to represent the Pure Land of Buddha in this world. At that time, I was in the beginning stages of coming into my beliefs and understanding of spirituality. The energy at the temple, which was undeniable, strengthened those beliefs. There was this overall zen feeling of peace and stillness that resonated with me in a way that made me question my movement tactics for the first time. The grounds were beautiful and unlike anything I'd ever seen. On the way out, I stumbled upon a souvenir shop selling small, rectangular handmade

Japanese plaques with different messages that represented different kinds of purposeful energy. There were plaques that were meant to support safety and protection while driving on the road. Still mourning Coco, my anxiety about driving was high because of her car accident. I thought there had to be some truth to this power. How else could I travel so far and, amongst all the souvenir shops and different plaques available, be drawn to this one? I knew immediately I wanted to bring that energy back home with me. So, I purchased a few plaques and gave them to family members who have cars. I didn't bring back many souvenirs from this trip, as I'd stopped buying souvenirs years earlier, but this felt right. Two years later, the plaques are still hanging below the rearview mirror in their cars, and I still believe in their protective power. That belief helps ease my anxiety so that I can continue to move forward, and I'm grateful for it.

After leaving Kyoto, I realized I forgot to empty my hotel safe. By the time I realized it, I was already on a bullet train to Tokyo. The safe had my Louis Vuitton loafers and two bottles of Tom Ford cologne in it, which, although valuable, wouldn't have been a big deal to lose. But my passport was also in the safe, and I definitely needed that to get back home. I was stressed thinking about the additional $300 and wasted time I would need to go back to Osaka and pick up my things from the safe. Luckily, I had international calling and data on my work cell phone. I was able to call the hotel, and though I struggled through the language barrier, they were able to open the safe with my code, get my items, and ship them to my hotel in Shinjuku, where I was staying for two days before relocating to a hotel in the Roppongi area of Tokyo for the remainder of my trip. By the time I arrived in Tokyo, fresh off the bullet train, my hotel was already aware of my situation and assured me that they'd let me know when my package arrived. In the end, everything worked out. It was a trip that was mirroring my life and foreshadowing a theme of faith that everything would be OK. It also reinforced in me that I could navigate unknown territory and solve any issues that would get thrown my way.

I ended up going on five more trips before the year was over, two of which were solo. I went to New Orleans; Montreal; Washington, DC; and Cartagena. I couldn't stop moving because I was afraid of what might happen if I did. It was my year of movement and I focused on healing by doing all the things I wanted to do.

Then, I got laid off from my job the following year in February 2019. I found myself on a budget with nothing but time. Movement looked a bit different now. Instead of traveling I threw myself into building a tech company. I built a web app from scratch, working fifteen hours a day, locked away in my apartment. I developed a business plan and a pitch deck that included branding and a comprehensive marketing plan. And when I was done, I had nowhere else to go. I had no money to take it any further. I had been rejected by every accelerator I applied to and every investor I reached out to. Due to the rejections, feelings of worthlessness—or like something was wrong with me— started to creep back in. I did everything I could and followed all the playbooks. It seemed like venture capitalists were throwing money at start-ups in Silicon Valley but even my Stanford connections couldn't get me anywhere. The only thing left for me to do was to double down on my healing efforts. I'd spent the previous year in therapy, while I was traveling at the same time, but my mind was still in turmoil, my heart still in pain. I no longer had the privilege of my employer-paid insurance and couldn't afford my therapist rates. So, it was up to me to use the tools I learned to continue my healing. I knew that if I was going to survive and be able to move my ideas forward, I needed to take the time to truly grieve and heal from all my trauma. I'd been running on E and purpose was the high-grade fuel I needed. So, I started writing with hopes of trying to organize my thoughts.

In my attempts to define my purpose, I realized that I wanted to help shift the paradigm of human nature. In my stillness it became clear to me how much we are evolving to look toward outside factors to satisfy our human nature: money, likes, status, etc. Losing love taught me that all we really need to live prosperous lives is love. Love is the foundation and everything else is secondary. Love is what we strived for before technology, and it will be what we strive for long after technologies fade. Matters of the heart can't be replicated, duplicated, or felt through any technology, no matter how much we try. Artificial intelligence might be the technology of the future and able to replicate and duplicate real intelligence. But love is spiritual, not binary. There's no such thing as "artificial love." In the words of Queen Mary J. Blige, "I'm searching for a real love." This will forever be the mantra of every human in this world, even for those reluctant to admit it to themselves. The lack of it causes pain, and people in pain tend to inflict pain on others. We go through life only meeting a handful of individuals. Our lives are short, and the world has almost eight billion people in it. Technology, however, allows the world to get to know us, which is why I've decided to show love to everyone I cross paths with. That's the legacy I want. Because who doesn't want love?

In the past, I aspired to acquire more money, likes, status, etc. It was that feeling of wanting more that caused me to lose sight of living in the moment; instead, I was living in bubbles of future states, that's where my dreams were. I was chasing the high of accomplishment and it became my normal. Gaining validation was my reward, but over time my losses started to accumulate, and my lows started gaining traction. Writing forced me to acknowledge the importance of my losses and how they have shaped me just as much as my wins. If I'd had a better relationship with the reality of loss, I think I would have tapped into its value earlier. I would've listened harder to the lessons even though I know they only matter to my psyche and my ego, which had unknowingly controlled my life. I've learned the hard way that rejection builds character and humility, even if it doesn't feel like it at the time. The yeses, however, display the reward for perseverance. Part of my healing work is constantly reminding myself that the amount of nos I've received is not as important as the times I received yeses because the yes is the defining moment. The nos are just the mess I have to crawl through to reach what's meant for me. It took time for me to internalize this and accept that the nos had nothing to do with my worth or ability.

Silently enduring loss after loss got to me though. It seemed like I was pursuing a dream only I could see. The losses felt like a personal attack on everything I knew to be true, like an attack on me. Trying to bring someone into my vision, one that I believed in wholeheartedly, was one of the hardest things to do and I didn't have a mental framework to manage all the rejections (job, business plan, programs, etc.). I wasn't prepared for it. We often hear success stories in the media about how someone got rejected thousands of times until they got the one yes that changed their life. However, there's not enough talk about the strain those thousands of rejections put on their mental health. Having an action plan is one thing, but every rejection hurts a little. You can endure them individually, but death by a thousand cuts is the worst kind. It's a life of suffering. I used to act like the rejections didn't faze me. I suppressed how it really made me feel until hurt overcame me. It weighed me down when all I wanted to do was take off. After Coco passed, the lows started to feel severely low and dark, and being low for too long made me start to question everything. But it was those questions that helped me become more myself.

WORTHINESS

For a long time I engaged in a push/pull relationship between survival and self-worth. Not consciously knowing or understanding my worth paved the way for clouds of fear and doubt to emerge, hindering my ability to see clearly. For me, the fear of leaving people behind became intense after Coco passed away. It was a fear I'd never felt enough to matter, but I now felt it with a striking intensity that paralyzed me. And there have always been people around me who never seemed to chase dreams the way I have, for reasons either within or beyond their control. Regardless though, I've always had to deal with their projections of possibilities. I can't count the times I've heard someone say to me, "Who do you think you are?" in an attempt to belittle my dreams or bring me back down to earth. I never let those kinds of comments stop me, but they always triggered some doubt and a decreased sense of worth because I wasn't clear on who I was. I didn't know who I wanted to be. I didn't have an answer for who I thought I was. Maybe they were right, and I was the crazy one. I can't sit here and say it never affected me, but it did push me because I knew I had to find out. I needed my answer to the question, "Who do I think I am?" The only way I was going to get answers was to go out into the world and try to find out. And that's what I've done over and over again, to figure out what's for me and what isn't. I was doing so with the mindset that eventually I would find my calling and find myself. When Coco passed, I found myself with no answers again. I wondered if my absence from my loved ones in pursuit of those answers was worth it.

Feeling worthy, I've come to find, is more than a mindset or an action. My sense of self-worth and self-love pierces through my veins and attaches to my bones. It wasn't like this before. Part of me thought I didn't deserve love because so many people that I loved were dying before I learned how to properly express my love for them. I always thought we'd have more time. So, I started anticipating people leaving, which forced me to put up walls to shield myself from the pain that would surely come. It made it hard for me to recognize and accept love. Money was a factor in my inability to break down those walls. I didn't have the money to take care of my ex girlfriend the way she needed to be taken care of, and that might've been the spark that caused a destructive feeling of inadequacy. There was this lingering reality that none of my accomplishments mattered much because they didn't amount to enough for her. She had her reasons for needing more, which I understood on some level, but it left me out. As a man living in a capitalist America, there's so much pressure in needing to be a provider, but my dad made it look easy. He's my example. I can't imagine having a family and not being able to come through for them in the way he always did for us, but I've also witnessed my dad give up his dream for us. I saw what that could do to a man. He went from DJing to being an artist, and his last attempt at pursuing his dream was in music. He managed a Harlem rap artist whom he believed in; ultimately, he succumbed to needing to financially support his family over his dreams. I knew I wasn't ready to give up on my dreams, especially because my dad's sacrifice gave me the room to dream. If only I could afford both love and the pursuit of my dreams.

It never dawned on me that I was worth all the love I was receiving. I couldn't get past my inability to give it back in the only way I knew how: by providing. For so long, I felt like I didn't have anything to provide. Too often I questioned my self-worth along my journey. I felt like a product of constant rejection. It was hard to figure out who I was as a young boy growing up in East Harlem. I often felt rejected when trying to be my authentic self. I wasn't into sports, hated violence, and didn't have much in common with the people around me. I thought it was a weakness. I always found myself fighting to prove I belonged, to prove I was worthy of love, attention, and acceptance. And sometimes the harder I fought to be myself, the harder the pushback I got whether in the streets, disagreeing with people's actions. Or at home, disagreeing with my parents. I found solace by retreating into myself. Being unapologetically myself became my reprieve from judgement.

WINNING ISN'T EVERYTHING

I had this vision of creating a new stock market; I realize the privilege in the audacity of that assertion. I won't go into details, but as one might imagine, this is a difficult thing to accomplish. However, I worked extremely hard to try and bring it to fruition, often getting very close as I brought people into my vision. The further I got in making this a reality, the harder it was to execute. My earned privilege could only take me so far and I was often met with no at the end of talks. It's scary attempting to create a system that could completely upend the way things have been done in an industry that hasn't had radical innovation in a long time. But my vision stemmed from history; with every new industrial era, we've seen markets spring up. There are markets where you can bet on the availability of oil, gold, oranges, etc. I was attempting to create a market where you can bet on digital media views. I had been trying to sell this idea since a pitch competition in 2011 during my last semester at Drexel. At the time, I didn't know how to bring all the pieces together to make it possible, but all my research suggested that theoretically it could be done. I didn't know everything; I just needed the right people to see the vision. It was the idea I submitted to work on during Stanford Ignite, but I would again be shut down, mostly because I still hadn't found the right way to present it so that people could understand. There were so many moving parts, but I would learn how to simplify the messaging through my education at Stanford. Using that knowledge, I fine-tuned my concept and was selected to be a finalist in the BNP Paribas Innovation Factory Competition, an internal competition for employees with innovative ideas. I began working at BNP Paribas in January 2017 as a consultant after I was let go from Natixis. The competition called for all employees from around the world to submit ideas to win access to bank resources for the development of their idea. The bank had over 100,000 employees and the competition would be narrowed down to just fourteen teams.

The leaders of the competition paired me with a partner to combine our ideas to create a comprehensive pitch geared toward engaging millennials in the stock market. Through my research, the only way I could see that happening was by creating a new stock market. My partner was in Paris at the headquarters while I was in the Jersey City office; most of our communication was via phone, email, or video conference. We did research, ideated, but we had fundamentally different views on what our final product should look like. I couldn't see past my vision. I genuinely felt that my idea was the better idea because of its radicalism. I've always been one to shoot my shot, no matter how insane, and I had the opportunity to at least pitch the idea to people who had the power to help me make it happen. My partner didn't feel the same. We were going in front of the executive committee of the entire bank and competing against colleagues from a myriad of different departments from across the globe and he didn't feel comfortable with the idea. He ended up dropping out two days before the presentation. In that moment, I had a choice to either drop out as well, give in to his ideas, or choose to present the idea myself. I'm not one to back down from a challenge, so I decided to present it myself. I wanted to win, and I felt stubbornly strong about my idea. But I didn't win. I hadn't factored in what my audience was looking for. They weren't looking for radical innovation; they were looking for simple innovation to improve their existing business. I wasn't upset about the decision, it just put things in perspective for me regarding corporate structure. I wouldn't have realized this perspective had I not put myself out there.

In spring 2018, I was in my year of movement, still trying to find ways to cope. I came across an Instagram influencer whom I'd been following for a while. I was drawn to his youthful but confident spirit and messaging on entrepreneurship. He was having a meetup in NYC one day, and I decided to go. It was a spur-of-the-moment thing. I had never done anything like it, but I needed to move and had nothing else planned that Sunday. The meetup was cool for nothing more than I met a lot of dope people, including a bright young woman who invited me to a weekend-long immersive workshop that her company hosted. It usually cost $300, but she gave me a free pass. The company was called Momentum Education, and it was designed to get you to become your best self. The weekend was the basic course with the theme of getting you to realize that what you don't know, you don't know. There were about eighty people attending the workshop, and I made connections with a few people over the course of the weekend. It became extremely personal, with people bravely sharing their stories and being vulnerable among strangers. I'd gone into the weekend open-minded with no real expectations for a breakthrough, but I knew it couldn't hurt and I was saying yes to all movement.

During one of the weekend activities, we played a game in which the class was divided into two teams: a red team and a black team with about forty players each. The facilitator laid out a set of rules we had to abide by in order to win the game; some were very technical and some were standard operational rules. Once I was assigned a team, I immediately went into competition mode, focusing on the big picture regarding getting the correct answers to questions. I wanted to win, but I had failed to see the real point of the game. There were only a few rules to the game but one in particular, the "make sure everyone in your team voted" rule, felt more like a technicality than a rule to be followed. We kept failing to advance to the next level. Every time we submitted our answers, we'd be met with a resounding fail and we couldn't figure out why. It wasn't until after several attempts that we found out what the problem was. The point of the game was not to just get the correct answer but to make sure everyone voted and had a voice in the decision-making process. We took votes when everyone wasn't even in the room. In the end, we all had to reflect on our personal parts played in the game. Did we sit back and let others make the decisions? Or did we step up and demand attention? I was part of the latter. I was so focused on winning the technical aspects of the game that I never even thought about everyone else. We had a captain—I wanted to be the captain but didn't win the votes—who didn't do a good job of rallying the team. I remember that's all I could think about.

I wanted to be the leader but didn't even realize that when we were holding votes, not everyone was physically in the room. Granted, it was a large number of people, but whether our answers were right or not, we'd never get the chance to advance to the next level. It made me think about leadership and how it's not a title to be appointed or won. I became aware enough to recognize that I relinquished any responsibility of rallying the team since I didn't win the title. After reflecting on the exercise, I also recognized my tunnel vision for winning. It was the only thing I could see and I couldn't help but think about how I had been moving through life with this same attitude. I was always focused on the win and getting to the light at the end was all I knew. I spent my life trying to reach certain goals. Failure was never an option. It's not something I thought about or processed as a possible reality. I was always too busy fig-uring out how to overcome whatever obstacle that presented itself. The need to win was a defense mechanism. If I could just win, I could prove myself. But, suddenly, three questions were hovering over me. What was I trying to prove? What were all the things I missed along the way? Who were all the people I neglected while being consumed with winning?

When I get obsessed about something, it's easy for me to get caught up in a rabbit hole of thoughts. That's what hap-pened to me after that weekend at Momentum. I started to feel guilty about things I never would have felt guilty about. My new widened view brought so much that I was missing into the frame and altered my perspective of some of the stories I'd been telling myself. And as much as I wanted to, I couldn't go back to redo situations with my new perspective in tow. Instead, I had to learn how to forgive myself for my past actions that I no longer agreed with. But the guilt was eating at me. The more I unveiled the things I missed out on in pursuit of getting a college degree, the more I started to feel as though my sacrifices were in vain. I felt like I hadn't accomplished enough for it to be worth it. This was furthest from the truth, but it was the story I began telling myself that aided my feelings of depression. My mind wouldn't allow me to believe anything different because for so long it based its values of worth on superficial metrics that I had grown to associate with the light at the end of the tunnel, like being a successful founder, having good credit, money in the bank, etc. I felt the most guilt about the time I missed out on with Raylin and Coco, pursuing a dream that might not come to fruition. The tunnel vision had caused me to miss so much, including time with my brother and the rest of my family.

The weekend at Momentum was eye-opening and its effects lasted well beyond the weekend. It was as if someone held a mirror to my face, and I could really see myself. It was the first time I really understood what it meant to be self-aware. Not only did the Momentum experience expose me to my flaws, but I had a wealth of experiences to dissect. I needed time.

YEAR OF STILLNESS

In the summer of 2019, I decided to take some time off from looking for work after being laid off from my role at Hedgserv. Being still proved to be just as ambitious an undertaking as any endeavor that involved mobility. It took a lot of work to be able to remove myself from the forward-thinking grind of my next achievement to just be. It took a lot of work to learn how to quell the anxiety that came with uncertainty so that I could revel in the certainty of my being. While I was upset about being laid off, I look back now and see that it was the best thing for me. I needed time and space to clean up my mental mess. I needed to organize my thoughts to gain clarity on what it is I should do next. I had no clue how long the process would actually take. I feel very privileged to have been able to take a year off from working for someone else so that I could work on myself. I think that if anyone ever gets an opportunity to take some time for themselves, they should do it. It could be a day, weekend, week, or year. I went from a year of movement when I went on six personal vacations to a year when I barely left my house. Taking care of me became my main priority. There was no amount of work, money, vacations, etc. that I allowed to interfere with that. I was way overdue on that kind of self-work and self-care.

Once I realized that I was my greatest asset, taking care of me became nurturing. I was the only one with insight into just what I needed when I needed it, and recognizing that was a game changer for me. It meant I no longer needed to look to outside factors for validation. I had to own this power to take the reins of my mental development, which became easier to grasp once I realized I was the only one who could, and everything I needed was already in me. I got to use my experiences as wisdom to facilitate making choices that were best for me. I chose happiness, no matter the situation. I chose forgiveness, no matter the betrayal, and I always chose love. However, even during this period of active healing, I sometimes didn't make the best choices for myself. I made the decision to forgive myself in these instances, and it elevated my enlightenment. I forgave myself for not trusting myself, for having doubt and fears, for relapsing into bad habits, and for failing. I forgave myself for all the mistakes I made in my creative, career, and personal pursuits. Deciding to forgive helped me normalize those doubts, fears, and self-mistrust by framing them as human reactions to vulnerability. As a Black man, I've often been told that vulnerability was a weakness. Therefore, I saw the doubt, fears, and self-mistrust that came from it as weaknesses, instead of reveling in my humanity.

Taking the time to gain a deep understanding of the triggers that prevented me from being vulnerable was a key part in my mastering my self-awareness. The stillness helped me recognize all the triggers that caused me to sabotage myself. Once I recognized the pattern, I then had to figure out why. I noticed that I subconsciously punished myself for not achieving a level of success I expected from myself. I could have compassion for others but not myself. For example, I always overeat. I tell myself I want to be healthy and fit, but I would often give into my cravings for comfort food and end up overindulging until I felt stuffed. I realized that I associated that stuffed feeling with security, especially when I was broke. Not knowing where my next meal would come from was a trigger for me that stemmed from constantly being in survival mode. My need for comfort food and feeling stuffed came from its association with financial security but also from conditioning placed on me when I was young.

I was born prematurely, a tiny baby that almost didn't make it, but it was God's plan. I was often overfed to make me grow, which normalized the feeling of being stuffed. My subconscious state of mind convinced me that this is how I should feel, despite always feeling extremely uncomfortable after overeating; discomfort was a punishment. I had to recognize my triggers and my conditioning to readjust my mindset around food. Being aware helped me begin to think twice every time I sat down to eat. I had to redefine what hunger meant to me and habitually remind myself of how I want it to be defined so that my brain could rewire its association with what it knew to be my point of fullness. Sometimes my subconscious mind would win, and I'd fall back into old habits that were detrimental to my health and fitness goals. It's why I always struggled with my weight but in those times when I would falter, I had to remember to be kind to myself. I had to remember that every time I slid back into those habits, I was moving the needle further away from achieving my goals. I was getting in my own way.

To stay focused on my goal of being healthy and fit, I had to tap into my "why." The superficial reasons, like looking good on a beach, no longer proved to be motivation enough. Now, one of the things I try and incorporate into my thinking around healthy eating and staying fit is my vision for a family. I know this might not come to fruition for a while since I'm still focused on my goal of becoming a successful entrepreneur, which means I won't have children until later in life. So, I made a pact with myself that since I was deciding to have children later, I must make sure I stay healthy and fit so that I can be energized when my family grows and can be in their lives for as long as possible. It went hand in hand. If anything did happen to me, I didn't want it to be because of a lack of effort on my part to take care of myself. After losing loved ones so early in life, I figured I owed it to them. Self-preservation was the least I could do. This framing gave me new purpose to keep going. I recognized my conditioning and knew it was within my power to choose to stay that path, to question it, and to unlearn it if need be. I was forced to question all of my beliefs to figure out what to face. This was a big part of my year of stillness, which I spent locked away in my room in my Harlem apartment, and then my parents basement, working on me. Some of the questions I asked myself were:

What do you believe about yourself?
What do you believe about your capabilities?
What do you believe about your faith?
What do you believe about your fears?
What makes you truly happy?
What do you believe about your life's purpose?

With these questions, I had to be brutally honest with myself. I had to find the courage to trust myself enough to know that

I was safe in the confines of my own mind and then be brave enough to write them down. The isolation helped me with this. I didn't have to worry about interjections from others. Once I answered these questions, the next step was to ask myself, Do these beliefs still ring true? Or was I holding on to this belief because it's all I've ever known? I'm as afraid of change as I am comfortable with it. It's why I would tend to stick to beliefs that no longer served me. I've experienced so much change that was out of my control. I thought staying true to my beliefs was a reprieve, but it was really doing more damage by not keeping up with what was going on around me. I was afraid of being someone different. I'd spent so long portraying a certain image of myself. What would that new me even look like? Would I recognize myself? Would others recognize me? Would they accept this new me? This is the narrative that was going on in my mind. I had to adjust, acknowledging that change can be growth with direction. It's evolution and it's our right as humans. Once we recognize and face our beliefs and who we are at any given moment, we can ask ourselves, Is this what I still believe today? Why do I believe this? And what do I want to believe about this? I knew that once I realized who I wanted to be, that's when the real work would begin. The follow-up must be action. I could never have imagined how much work actually goes into this process or how long it would take. To get rid of those old habits, thoughts, and beliefs, I needed to define and constantly reaffirm my new ones. I did this every day until I stood firm in who I was, not who I was becoming. I had to actively keep my new beliefs top of mind, no matter what else was going on in my life. It's why the stillness was so important for me as I was able to focus. It wasn't easy, but I love the version of myself that emerged after the work was done. Growth requires sacrifice. I had to sacrifice the old me to grow into the new me.

Toward the end of my year of stillness, when I moved into my parents' house, it felt akin to the end of 'The Alchemist' by Paulo Coelho, one of the many books that I'd read to help me through my journey, when he returned home to find the love he'd traversed the earth in search of was there all along. Suddenly, spending time with my family became my favorite thing to do. It was as if a whole new world opened for me. We were learning the new versions of each other that had been shaped and molded based on our individual experiences as well as our collective ones, including our shared grief. We reconnected with each other. I wanted to hold on to them for as long as possible, as I knew it was temporary and I wouldn't be staying with them forever. So I made it a priority, finding things we could do together, like my mom and I joining forces to complete a juice cleanse, ridding our bodies of toxins, and ascending to the same wavelength where we acknowledged our bodies as temples.

My parents have always been there whenever I needed them. Moving in with them helped remind me of their unconditional love for me, which helped set the bar for me building unconditional love within myself. No matter how much we argued or disagreed, they always came through for me when it really mattered. I believe my father's instinct regarding his children is to first offer pushback, which helped to strengthen me and my brother's resolve. At the same time, I can attribute my dauntless courage in taking risks to knowing that if I fall, he'll be there to help me back up. That's love. That's family. We do what we need to do for each other when it's most important even if it's inconvenient. Love is reserved for those who show up. Love shows up. It's hard to show up as much as you'd like when you're on a personal quest though. When I left for college, I had a whole world open to me, which meant less time to be with my family. In my stillness, I was discovering that life, like a song, is as good as the harmony of its melodic parts.

ROCK BOTTOM

Living with my parents during this half of my stillness created a safe space for me to explore the depths of the sadness and grief I was feeling. I wanted to feel all of it and I let myself get as low as possible. There was a small part of me that could've stopped myself, but I became addicted to the sadness. It became an unhealthy challenge to see how low I could go. How much pain could I endure? It was my way of dealing with the immense guilt that I felt over not being a better brother, cousin, son, friend to those that I loved and for choosing my own ambitions over spending precious time with loved ones before it was too late. I realized I reached rock bottom when I was having those thoughts of wanting to give up on life. The sadness had become unbearable, and I got to a point where I couldn't bring myself out of it no matter how much I wanted to. I thank God for my mom who made sure to always check up on me during the stillness. She was the constant presence in my life that I needed when everything seemed uncertain. I never talked to her about how I was feeling because I didn't want to burden her. I didn't want to burden anyone and kept these feelings to myself.

Hitting rock bottom was serious, more serious than I'd ever thought, which I didn't realize until I tried to get back up and couldn't. It went beyond my emotions and mental health. It was like everything came crashing down at once. The weight of losing Coco, my job, and later my apartment in Harlem because of somehting out of my control seemed unbearble. It was like my life wasn't mine. Even my apartment which was my safe space that I customized to maximize my healing efforts was taken from me. I was thirty-one and had to move into my parent's basement again because I wasn't working. I had to laugh because I never would have thought that I'd be physically back in my parents' home, needing their help, and alone again. I often thought that I didn't have anyone to talk to about my depression but that wasn't true. I just chose not to talk to people about what was going on with me. For a long time, I was afraid to ask for help. There was a certain image I portrayed about myself that was centered around strength. How would being open about my struggles disrupt that image? I didn't want to find out but then I couldn't keep it in anymore.

I was beginning to feel very lost. I felt like all my efforts were in vain, and I couldn't see a way forward. But I remembered how talking about what I was going through helped me. Right before I was laid off and the end of my year of movement, I remember thinking about what it would be like to end it all. Wanting the pain and I felt to stop. I called my cousin Andrew and he talked me down off the mental ledge. I also ended up confiding in one of my close friends Gabriel, ironically at happy hour one day after work. I wasn't planning on it, but I felt compelled to in the moment and his support meant everything to me. It gave me the courage to really start opening up and being more vulnerable. Which I needed if I was going to get through this. My cousins and friends showed up for me when I needed it, and I will always be grateful to have them for that. Initiating those conversations was the beginning of me taking ownership of my feelings although I'd have a long road after that. It felt like a weight being lifted off my shoulders, creating space for me to think about how to heal during this phase of stillness I was in, when there was no where else to run.

Ironically, for as long as I can remember, the pursuit of my safety always kept me on the edge of a cliff. I always seemed to thrive on the edge. I knew that pursuing my dreams was a risk. I constantly took leaps with some of the decisions I made, hoping it would all work out for the best, and believing in myself enough to know that if it didn't, I could bounce back (this happened often along my journey). But there was something different about this seemingly never-ending fall I found myself in. It seemed like nothing was working out in my favor. I knew the superficial losses, like my job and apartment, were temporary so I wasn't angry about that, a little dissapointed though. But I knew that I'd built an elevator on my way up for this very reason, to cushion a fall so I'd never have to start from scratch. My experience and knowledge were cemented and nothing or no one could take that from me. But after losing my job, I had nothing but time to think. I couldn't escape all the things I was running from, which intensified feelings of grief. It all came rushing to the forefront of my mind and I wanted to make it stop. I didn't want to feel the pain I was feeling anymore. I had to figure out how to recover from this, and fast. Ending my life, once again, became a potential solution in my mind, so I bet myself that I could heal myself and become better than I was before. That was my newest challenge to become the best version of me and unlock the next level that involves emotional and spiritual stability. These were elements of safety that I never thought to pursue. Making deals with myself is how I got through a lot of things. When I took out my first loan for college, I promised myself that I would make the most of it and do whatever it took to pay it off, a promise I'm still working hard to keep.

At the start of this newest challenge to heal myself I went back into my notes from therapy sessions to get some tools I might have forgotten about. And I was a regular at the book store, reading through as many self help books as I could. I quickly recognized that I had to learn how to love myself. To make that love louder than any thoughts could cause me harm. So, I put self-love in the context of what I understood most. I spent over a decade in the business and technology industry and at my core I felt that I understood the concept of an investment better than anything else, delaying instant gratification to reap higher rewards at a future time. This is a concept I understood in monetary theory and business but rarely practiced in my personal life. I often gave in to instant gratification, as if the feeling amounted to the love I craved but wouldn't allow myself to have. After all, I'd spent a decade studying business, not love. I needed to invest in learning how to love myself unconditionally. Most of my personal investments had been educational in nature, but I had to approach this differently. I'd done enough research to know that it was an investment that would have a high return if executed properly. Once I got a better understanding of what self-love is, and more importantly what it looked like for me, I began to fall in love with myself in a way that I'd never felt before. I let go of any idea of perfection and embraced being a perfectly imperfect person. I needed to grow my belief that in every moment and every situation, I had done my best with the information available to me. I had to bring that understanding of life to the surface. Reflecting helped me see that, good or bad, I've always made decisions based on the information I had, my perfectly flawed emotions, and the enhancement of my understanding of what it truly means to be human.

GOING INWARD

When I was in doubt about my worth, I had to be louder about my pain, joy, and my truths, even if I was just speaking to myself. In fact, especially when I was speaking to myself. That became my strategy for building myself back up even if I didn't fully believe the things that I was saying yet. I had to alter my inner voice when I realized how habit-forming the way I spoke to myself was. I had to understand that the power of what I told myself didn't come overnight. I had to be disciplined. After reading *The Power of Habit* by Charles Duhigg, I gave myself grace, allowing time for my mind to accept the new positive affirmations I was telling myself. I had to break the habit of defaulting to self-destructive thoughts. To do that, I had to figure out what perceived reward I was gaining for self-destruction thoughts. Through this process, I learned that consoling the guilt I felt for being alive was the reward I gained from the habit of self destructive thoughts.

Learning to be positively louder and trusting my inner voice was the engine that drove my healing. And as I continued to be truly open with myself I found healing to get smoother. Practicing on myself was the best way for me to learn how to open up to others. It offered up my deepest sincerities and enhanced my ability to empathize. But it wasn't easy. I'd built walls so thick that trying to break them down was exhausting. However, I committed to getting better mentally, so I had to do the work. Every evening I chipped away at those walls and writing was the best tool for this process. There's something unexplainably therapeutic about writing down your thoughts. Then came the pattern of stopping and starting as I got close to breaking a wall down, often sabotaging demolition day. Being on the cusp of changing who I was and how I thought and being aware of the change as it happened created resistance from my old self who didn't want to let go. Eventually, I had to submit to the voice I wanted to prevail. Every time I broke down a wall, I realized, it was not so bad on the other side.

This progressively grew my confidence. I would think to myself, *What were you so afraid of?* Once I figured it out, I thought about the root cause, which often stemmed from something negative in my childhood. It often took some time though, requiring me to intentionally target and break down even more walls. Overcoming those internal blockages always resulted in new perspectives for me. I found clarity with my issues that allowed me to release the weight of the walls I was holding up and ease any mental tension that would cause me distress so that I could move on to the next issue. It became what seemed like at times a never-ending cycle. I often go back to issues I thought I'd let go of. But when I do, I notice it's alway a little easier to dig deeper within myself about how how I truly feel and about how an issue or trauma has affected me and my decision making. I looked back on what I thought then, acknowledged my role and why I reacted the way I did in any given situation, then I'd acknowledge what I currently believe and why, accepting and taking any wrongdoings on my part. As my voice grew louder, my inner warrior grew fearless of what was beyond the walls I had put up. I had to let my inner warrior out on D-Day. D-Day is a stream of conciousness that occurs when

I'm ready to destroy any perspectives or thought proccess that didn't serve a healed version of myself. That was my main goal of my inward journey. To come out healed so I could thrive in pursuing the dreams I held for myself.

Going inward allowed me to really feel what it's going to take to accomplish my goal of becoming a successful entrepreneur. It allowed me to understand the risks and what I might need to sacrifice to get there and, consequently, made me very aware that I wasn't ready to take on that role yet. I couldn't confidently walk into my purpose until I healed from all the traumas in my past and demolished all the walls that were blocking my way of executing the how I needed to. The insecurities, fear, and all the other negative stories I told myself had to go, and I had to figure out how to make that happen. There was no room for those things and my dreams to manifest simultaneously. This healing journey has allowed me to drum up so many of the traumatic things in my life and analyze them and understand my underlying emotions and bring them to the surface to face them. It helps me be aware of myself when I feel those emotions again in any present moment. I can recognize it as a recurring emotion that was automatically triggered as a reaction to the trauma. This is how I recognized that my bad habits were so dangerous, especially when mixed with a lack of self-awareness. I found that simply being in a headspace to actively recognize when I was having an emotional reaction to something allows me to quickly course correct my response and actions to reflect my current stance on the issue and not what I've been wired to do based on a past trauma. That kind of power over myself became intoxicating and strengthened my instincts. You can always manipulate someone who isn't aware of themselves because you can drum up emotions just by figuring out their triggers and hitting them whenever you need to. I understand this because I've been manipulated enough times to recognize the pattern.

Emotional warfare is real. I no longer wanted to be powerless over myself. I wanted to shield myself against the old, naive me. It became a battle. Two sides of me and each side was fighting to win. I finally realized that the best course of action was just to blend the two to make one, and that would be the whole version of me with all sides existing at the same time. It's the skill of acute awareness that made the difference. If I did something that made me feel smart, then I'd relish in the euphoric feeling of accomplishment. What I now know is that if I feel dumb ten minutes later because of something I didn't know, then that's OK too. The awareness here is making sure I don't beat myself up about it. Failure of any kind was a huge trigger for my self-destructive habits. Instead, I decided to be happy about feeling dumb, about failing. It meant that I now had the opportunity to learn something new; there was a lesson to be found in the experience of failing. No one was meant to know everything anyway, right?

If I'd found myself happy and then something happened that made me angry, I learned to be OK with the anger and the shift away from the happiness I'd been feeling. I recognized anger as a natural human emotion. It was when the anger unconsciously held power over me that it was detrimental. I had a choice in those angry moments. I could let my anger control me, or I could be in control of my anger. I now understand more than ever how that choice will always dictate my next course of action. It's a decision that no one can make for me. I know now that whatever choice I make doesn't just affect me, it affects everyone around me. Angry decisions never led me toward my goals and will always be counterproductive. My self-awareness helped me gain control over my anger so that I could choose wisely in my decisions throughout my day-to-day life. My self-awareness has allowed me to be forward thinking and quickly take action whenever something happened to me that was out of my control. It's a daily practice that takes time and effort to master. But I aim to get out of my head and spend more time being present.

THE BURDEN OF CURIOSITY

Throughout my college and corporate career, I've been able to create an intense focus that allows me to drill down and get my work done. The more I did, the more I uncovered how much more there was to learn and do. Growing up in East Harlem, I can't remember having a platform that allowed me to explore my curiosity. But as soon as I got to Drexel, it exploded. There was so much I didn't know and so much to do that I never knew was an option that I dove headfirst into exploration. There was always something to learn or do. This led me to often feel that showing up for others was taking away from time I needed to satisfy my curiosity and the work it would take to do so. It meant I had to slow down, and that went against everything I thought I knew. I would get so aggravated whenever I planned out my day and it got thrown off course because of someone or something out of my control. I would always adapt and adjust my schedule accordingly, but it got under my skin. I never thought that my time was more valuable than anyone else's, but it was always hard to get others to understand my drive and ambition; I didn't even understand my drive and ambition and I damn sure couldn't control it. In order to accomplish everything I needed to, I would have every minute accounted for, even my rest time. To afford this ambitious lifestyle, I came to rely on convenience. Any little thing to make my life easier and carve out more time to work was a blessing. I often viewed taking the time to show up for others as an inconvenience. I always showed up, but it was often more out of a sense of obligation than desire, which is ironic because I used to feel that people only showed up for me out of obligation, especially my father. I realize now that I was just projecting my issues onto him. As I got older, I realized more and more that being there for my loved ones is a priority goal for me. It's the thing I want most. My year of stillness has taught me how to use patience to better manage my ambition so I can make time for the people that I love. If it's not love, I don't have time for it.

They say men tend to end up like their fathers. In general, we become mirror images of our parents. How could we not if we spend our formative years being conditioned by them, often with little regard to the development of our individual perspective. It's why I see parenting as very difficult and one of the reasons I haven't started my own family yet. I needed more understanding of life and its immense possibilities first.

In the Black community, I've often witnessed the disregard of children's perspectives, masked in colloquialisms such as "Because I said so," and "Stay in a child's place." Following orders seems to be the main parenting skill that's made its way through generations since slavery. I've seen this style of parenting turn abusive, producing rebellious children who too often turn into unstable adults. This is the type of traumatic generational cycle that we've accepted as the Black experience. A way of life that we turn into our culture. A culture that oftern perpetuates the dangers of the world for Black boys and girls. So we continue to force our children into submission just to keep them safe, to quell their curiosity enough to ensure their safe return home. I've asked myself, is it worth it? For a long time, I didn't think it was. It caused such a strain on my relationship with my father because I couldn't understand why he treated me like a soldier instead of a curious child. During my teenage years, I was always angry with him. The wildfire in me wanted to burn and he kept extinguishing my flame; he kept me alive though. I wanted to run the streets but at a young age, in an environment where everyone else was outside, I couldn't understand why I couldn't be. Instead of talking to me, for the most part, all I got was "Because I said so." I hated that. I didn't have an alternative outlet for my curiosity about the outside world that I thought I was missing out on. I could deal with the no if I knew why. I hated not having an explanation. So, I stopped asking. I couldn't continually have my curiosity shut down in disappointing blows. I hated the child's place and I hated that I couldn't effectively communicate how I felt about it with my father.

I was living the Black experience but with a military dad who had a military dad, which made my disciplined upbringing more intense. We always had to present ourselves a certain way. We couldn't leave the house with a single wrinkle on our clothes. We were always cleaning the house from top to bottom with inspections of even the tiniest crevices. My dad was in the U.S. Navy. He had been out before I was born so I only heard the stories of his time serving our country. My dad's dad was in the U.S. Army and served during World War II. The mix of discipline, tough love, and being Black was at the heart of these tensions with my dad. It made me hate discipline or any form of authority that instructed me to value the word of anyone over what I needed for myself. Like most teens, all I wanted was my independence. I was curious about the world and felt trapped by the confines of the hood, as well as my father's idea of who or what I should be.

Now that I'm a grown man, I think about how I would raise my kids. The first thing that comes to mind is: help them find their passion. I'd like to think that mixing discipline with passion will help them thrive, not just survive. I've found that when I'm passionate about a subject, I'm more committed to seeing it through to fruition. Passion breeds discipline, but discipline alone cannot instill passion. This is why I want to promote tapping into our authentic selves more; I believe the love of life it produces can overpower any obstacle.

Once I realized I wanted better answers, I knew I would have to get them for myself. This is part of how my independence was formed. This was the making of an entrepreneur. I never stopped asking questions. I just had to find resourceful ways to get answers. My summer at Columbia during high school was when I fully understood that the caliber of answers varied dramatically based on where or who I was getting them from. It led me to develop an intolerance for mediocre answers that never satisfied my curiosity or challenged me to be better. I wanted to learn from the best of the best. I think about today's generations of youth who've become infinitely curious with the rise of the Internet where they can gain access to answers in seconds. They don't necessarily have to go through the long and arduous process of traditional education. They're demanding answers and breaking stifling generational habits in their quest to get them. The problem I'm noticing though is that they're accepting mediocre answers and even factually incorrect ones. I believe that our society, as a whole, must demand better answers and higher-quality solutions from our leaders. The modern quagmires that plague us require them. Great things take time and can't be figured out with a quick search. Knowledge is a prerequisite for wisdom. But, with the influx of inaccurate information posing as knowledge, I wonder if technology is raising a generation of youth who will grow old but not wise. If so, what will the repercussions be when it's time for them to lead?

My curiosity has been a major key to my success. I love learning, and once I learn about something, I dig deep to understand it as best I can. If I learn something new on my last day of life, I'd die happy. I just hope it's not something new about myself. I want to know myself as deeply as possible when I go. Part of coming into adulthood for me is really understanding how short life is. So, during my time of stillness, I made it a daily habit to tell myself who I am, to check in, and remind myself as soon as I wake up, "You Are a King." If my life ever gets taken from me, I want to die fully aware of my power, wielding it until my last breath.

FINDING ALLAH

As a young man growing up, I was never able to fully accept the concept of a Black church because the times I did make it to church even though the audience was Black, the religion that was being preached was white, and I couldn't understand or trust any form of worshipping a white man. Especially being named after legends who made it their life mission to fight against the tyranny of white men toward black men. Especially when I was living under the oppressive thumb of white men.

One weekend in August 2018, during my year of movement, I drove up to Montreal with a couple of my coworkers. We were three guys from completely different backgrounds exploring a new city and all it had to offer. We stopped in this grandiose Catholic church that we stumbled upon while walking through the city. The opulence alone made me feel uncomfortable. Then the preacher started talking about blood sacrifices. It was so off-putting, I had to get up and leave. The ideals that were being presented felt very cultish, and there's nothing wrong with that. I know that there are people who truly believe in the Catholic Church. But I wasn't one of them.

My journey to spirituality started around the same time I began regularly going to therapy to try to be more present and quell my anxiety. Therapy was an important part of my journey to healing because it was the start of my process of looking inward. It's weird that we need help to look inside ourselves, but I honestly had no idea where to even begin. I spent a large part of my life building up walls so that I would never have to. Black men have been told for decades that this was the right way to be. We keep everything inside, but it's so damaging that we must start breaking this cycle of unhealthy masculinity. What I've learned is that there's a science to getting out of your own way. And there's an art to embracing your full self: the good, the bad, and the ugly.

It took a while for me to really open up to my therapist; I'd say a good four to six months. Most of the conversations in our hourly sessions were very surface level, but he never pressured me. After every session, he'd often leave me with a question to think about based on what we discussed. It was always as if he knew exactly what to say to get me to think deeper. Our sessions were usually on Friday evenings after work and then I'd end up spending the entire weekend in my head. I often passed on social engagements so that I could analyze what we talked about and find answers to the questions he posed. There had to be answers to his questions, right? I just had to figure them out. It was in this work outside of therapy where my true healing began. I isolated myself from the rest of the world during these times. I needed as much time as possible to chip away at the walls that were preventing me from reaching my answers. I needed to be alone to confront what I was avoiding. Whatever came from it, whatever trauma I had to uncover, could be done in the safety of my own space without judgment from anyone. I had to learn how to be vulnerable. Ironically, I couldn't do that around other people. Now, I'm very comfortable with being vulnerable around others because I accept all of me. But it took a lot of work to get to this level of comfortableness with myself.

Part of these weekends of exploration included trying to isolate certain feelings to pinpoint their origin, to slowly allow myself to be completely honest with myself regardless of how it made me feel. Meditation was a way to help me focus my thoughts. I always thought ten steps ahead, never actually taking in the moments I was in, which made it harder for me to target the traumatic experiences that were subconsciously guiding how I lived my life.

What I unexpectedly found was that when I meditated, I experienced a new kind of energy that I had never felt before. It was as if the universe opened a door for me to walk through, a portal into a new dimension that filled me with light and energy. I found myself suddenly understanding what people meant by the term "vibrate higher." It was intoxicating. The energy that I felt was soulful and sparked my interest in spirituality and the idea of a higher being. I felt it. And for me, that made it real. It was undeniable that there was an energy frequency around me that existed beyond my daily comprehension, moving throughout the universe aloof until I tapped in.

At first, the meditation process seemed like chaos. I could only sit still for about one minute, breathing in and out to try to calm my mind, but then it felt like the room was spinning. I knew I couldn't give up though. I wanted to unlock the benefits that I'd read and heard about from others. I knew that if I could be disciplined enough in the practice I would get there. My breathwork started with a simple count. I'd breathe for a count of four, hold in for a count of four, then exhale for a count of four and repeat. A technique I'd read about online. It wasn't until I was able to sit still and focus on breath work for about five minutes that I started to feel like I had some control over the energy that spiraled around me. I equated the feeling with my depressive mindset, chaotic and out of my control. With constant practice, I was able to calm my mind. It was no longer racing, and I was able to feel mentally balanced, affirming a divine order. By the time I was able to meditate for ten minutes at a time, I could no longer ignore the overwhelming feeling of being tapped into an energy frequency that I'd never felt in my life. And I knew I wanted to live within that frequency. It made me feel connected to a higher power. It made me feel in control and powerful.

The next question I had to ask myself is, What does that higher power look like? I had never been into religion. I didn't believe in it. Mostly I thought that religion preyed on individuals who were going through hard times. I looked at it as being weak. Really, I hated being told what I could and could not do. I struggled with submission of any kind. In my mind, that's not what men did (a mindset that's a testament to my East Harlem upbringing). I'm a rule breaker by nature, so organized religion never appealed to me. I would much rather create my own set of values and beliefs. I had been scarred seeing family members completely relinquish control over their lives and flip on who they were and what they believed. I always believed in God or a higher power, even though I had never really felt it. I never took the time to ask myself why. It was most definitely blind faith. It was status quo to believe in God. My recent decision to explore religion came after I started to spiritually feel connected to God and wanted guidance on life. I needed it in fact. I was going through hard times. I developed a new understanding of faith and its endurance during the hardest test of my life. Faith became easy when it was all I had left.

I've always had issues asking for help when I needed it. I usually waited until situations became dire to seek it out. It's my independent nature. My mindset was always that I had to make it on my own. My dad used to always say to me, "You're not going to be grown and living with me, so you better figure it out." He had ten brothers and sisters, a good portion of whom lived with their parents until they died. He only had two kids, but I understand now how the trauma of that experience weighed on him enough for it to be projected onto me. I'm sure the last thing he wanted was a forever-dependent child. I didn't understand it as a kid though. It made me believe I had no other choice than to make it on my own. It was a narrative he preached when we were poor. Over time our circumstances changed, elevating to middle-class poor; my conditioning, however, had not. After feeling God's presence, I wanted to learn how to connect with him more to recognize his guidance. Learning how to submit to his will and ask him for help opened up a new way of life for me, one where I didn't want to go at life alone ever again. I prayed that God would always be there with me.

Something was always off about Christianity to me. It was the worship of another human that I could never understand. Being named after Malcolm X, I had some introduction to Islam but not a lot. So, I decided to do some research by listening to some of his speeches and reading as much as I could. What stood out to me the most was that to worship Allah is to worship the highest power, the creator of our universe. I learned that Elijah Mohammad, just like Jesus Christ, was a prophet, a messenger. I found solace in that. It helped me become comfortable with the idea of worship and giving up control to something that was above all humans. If I were to become Muslim though, would I adhere to all the rules? My increasing spirituality and connection to a higher power was what opened me up to the idea of religion. My thoughts were scattered about it though. I didn't need or want to be controlled. I thought I could never completely surrender myself to the ideals of another human, prophet or not. For all I knew, I could be a prophet. Why are my beliefs less valid when they're God-given? Becoming Muslim meant that I had to accept Muhammad as the last prophet. Who wants to be a prophet anyway? So much pressure.

I began to study Islam with the notion that I'd use the teachings as a guide to help me define my core values. There were things I agreed with wholeheartedly and things I did not. As an innovator, I'm a strong believer in modern amendments. With the advancements that we have today, we can no longer base our way of living on ideals from centuries ago. We must adjust to fit our current way of life. So, that's what I did.

The first time I went to a mosque was a great experience. I approached a colleague at work, who I knew was Muslim, about where he went to worship. At this point, I was very close to making my decision to become Muslim. He invited me to come along with him to a mosque that he went to every Friday during his lunch break, and I eagerly accepted. I wanted to get the experience of worship within the Islamic community. I had a lot of experience in Christian and Catholic churches but never a mosque. The energy in the mosque sold me. It felt honest and pure. There was no opulence at all. The entire service was about protecting the rights of education for children, especially for young girls, and how important it was to challenge old ideals and create safe spaces for young girls to thrive. The message was timely, positive, and sincere, which seemed to be in direct contrast to what I had experienced in other places of worship. At the time, I didn't know much about Islam but the more I researched, the stronger the connections I felt to Allah. This was a connection I'd never felt in my attempts at worshiping the image and idea of Jesus.

But what about my life outside of Islam? I decided that I would continue to celebrate holidays such as Christmas. If Islam recognizes and embraces Jesus Christ as a prophet and messenger, then He should be celebrated. I believe that celebrating and worshiping are two different things. This approach for me exemplifies my belief in unity and how we can all exist together. I don't believe humans were created to be restricted. Humans created restrictions to be imposed on other humans for the benefit and gain of "select" humans. Christmas is a holiday that I've celebrated my entire life. It honestly wasn't so much about religion as it was about family and coming together to express our gratitude and love for one another. But when it comes to my faith, I feel as though I was selected by Allah through some kind of divine intervention that led me to him. It made the validation of other humans feel less significant. I decided to live by my rules, with guidance from the teachings of Islam. Experiencing so much loss made me realize just how precious life is, and I want mine to be as fulfilling as possible.

One of the hardest thing I ever had to do was get out of my own way. I try and focus on the things that are within my control and ability. This way I leave little room for another human to get in my way. I am, however, always open to debate. When it comes to relion I'm by no means a expert and I will never proclaim to be, but it's a journey. A very new to me, but I'm constantly learning. And I know that's all I can do. My only purpose in even expressing what I've come to believe in this moment is to offer my defense as reasonable doubt against what society has come to accept as true regarding divisiveness amongst humans.

I try to make it a point to thank God daily. I'm not at a point where I complete full prayers five times a day but I proclaim, "Allaahu Akbar," constantly. Once I put my anxiety in the context of me resisting the need to give up control of the future, I realized the resistance came from not having a place to put it. When I asked Allah for help, he responded by taking my worries away. That was the benefit of submitting to this higher power, whether it was a plan for the next hour, day, or year. The lesson I had to learn over and over was that I cannot control anything but my actions at any given moment. We can't go back to the past and we can't forecast future outcomes. The fact of the matter is that no human can, no matter how much we like to think differently. I surrendered to a life in the present and the idea that prayer and hard work would steer me toward the things I wanted with hopes that Allah would meet me halfway. Preparation became my tool to help defeat anxiety. I knew I had to put myself in positions to receive Allahs blessings, whatever they may be. I had to put my worry in his hands. I had to become super aware of myself to ensure that in moments of uncertainty, I made decisions that aligned with my beliefs and the vision of my life that was gifted to me by Allah.

HEALING FROM GRIEF

I never got to say goodbye to Raylin and Coco. Not truly. I couldn't let them go. It never even occurred to me that I had to. I'd been to so many funerals in my life and saying goodbye became so desensitized, it was more procedural than spiritual. Saying goodbye to my cousins meant saying goodbye to a part of myself that had been conditioned for forever, which is why I was doing the opposite. I was fighting to keep them with me. As much as I was used to change, I couldn't picture my life without them. Then I wondered if I felt guilty about not letting them go. How could they rest in peace if I didn't? Was this guilt causing me to inflict pain on myself as punishment? I don't think that was my intent, but subconsciously it was possible. I don't understand how we, as humans, continue to hurt ourselves. We must do better. There came a point where I realized that I didn't want to live the rest of my life in pain. I want to live in love. I felt that love was the light at the end of my tunnel. "Rest in Peace" suddenly held a new meaning for me. For either of our souls to be at peace, we had to let each other go. That's what love does. I love them and I love me.

When we were young, Raylin and I had a conversation about being each other's best man at our weddings. To this day, I grapple with the idea of getting married and not having him there. I have a lot of good male friends, but the idea of making any of them my best man feels like a betrayal to Raylin. After he passed, for a long time any form of intimacy with a male friend felt like betrayal, like I was searching for a replacement to fill the void. I distanced myself from the idea. I buried myself in work so there'd be no time or opportunity to reach that level of intimacy. My work didn't fill the void though. It took a while to accept the fact that nothing ever would and that it didn't mean I had to deprive myself of love or intimacy. I could let someone get to know the real me without diluting my and Raylin's relationship. In some ways though, to know me is to know Raylin. Anyone that comes into my life now will never get that chance to know me on that level. I fear, for that reason, there will always be this existential barrier between me and whoever comes into my life who did not know him. For a long time, he took up a majority of the space I had inside, but holding on to him and his memory got harder and harder as time went by. There was no room to let anyone else in. That meant I had to give up more of his space. Letting him go helped me gain capacity. Immortalizing him in this book helped me be OK with that.

There's a part of Raylin that I didn't know too well, partly because he hid it from me and partly because I didn't want to see it. I didn't really know him as "Carter," the nickname given to him for his love of Shawn "Jay-Z" Carter. Part of the reason it took me so long to let go of him is that I was searching for signs of Carter, the man he was when he took his last breath. I blamed myself for being disconnected from him at the time, for not knowing to pause my ambition, pull over to the side, and notice everything around me beyond the tunnel vision I'd immersed myself in. I didn't understand how the impact of a year or two of coming into your own could completely transform a person. Those who knew me before my healing process, doesn't know me now. There were so many changes going on in my life. I was living in two different worlds. I'd often hear that I should not change or forget where I come from. I'm not sure why Black people glorify this idea of equating being "real" with staying the same when life is about growth. No one should ever stay the same. When I think about it though, that rhetoric often comes from people who can't or won't change, as a way of keeping you attached to their comfort level.

Every summer, we held a memorial for Raylin in Roy Wilkins Park in Queens, NY. The year that Coco passed, we decided to combine memorials for them. It was there that Bernard, a close family friend that was like a cousin to us, told me a story about Raylin, really about Carter. I tried to envision it, but I couldn't. It was out of character for the Raylin I knew. I just took Bernard at his word. Bernard was with Raylin the day he died. He was also shot but survived. His survival changed the nature of our relationship for me. I felt a range of emotions from anger to jealousy within me. I still have a hard time putting into words how I felt. Even after the five years in prison he served I couldn't bring myself to latch on to our past relationship. He was out, living his life, telling me stories about Raylin. It didn't seem fair. He died to me that day as well. It was easy to blame him when I had no outlet for my grief. But healing helped me understand that blame just continues a cycle of hurt. Later that night, after the memorial, I'd gone home alone to the safe space I created for myself in my apartment in Harlem. I was laying on my bed feeling sad when all of a sudden Raylin's spirit came to me in a truly out-of-body experience. I relived the entire story that Bernard told me from Raylin's perspective. I could see what he saw, feel what he felt, and I acted it out as him.

I jumped out of bed as soon as this invisible force inhabited my entire being. I was no longer in control of my ligaments or my consciousness. It felt like what I'd imagine a seance would feel like. It was powerful yet subtle. There was no Big Bang, just me as Raylin. I knew it the moment I felt this fearlessness flow through my veins, an energy reminiscent of his essence. It was a moment of intimacy that reinforced our connection, sans the physical but cosmically spiritual. It was an energy that I'd never felt before. I reveled in it as I took on his spirit, re-creating this scene from his life with a vision muddied by a fog that separated dimensions of past and present. I hated what I saw, but the fearlessness was intoxicating. Was this the same fearlessness that led to Raylin's death? Was the purpose of this experience motivational or cautionary? I liked my ignorant bliss.

In that moment, I was reminded just how fearless he was and how, because of him, I know what it feels like to be fearless. I always knew he was brave though, and I got that trait from him, one of the greatest gifts I've ever received. I just needed a reminder. The sadness, shock, and guilt of being alive caused me to become so confused about what I knew about myself and about our relationship. I'd lost confidence in myself and let fear take over. I couldn't let him go until we were squared away, but a part of me thought we'd never be squared away. That was the guilt that ate at me. I thought about what he would have accomplished today if he had gotten the chance to continue harnessing his fearlessness for his betterment, something he was in the middle of doing. We were going to take over the world together. He knew how to live life. I suppose he's where I get that from as well. I had to come to terms with the fact that his purpose here was served. I felt sad by this revelation but I also felt grateful that I had the opportunity to be a part of his purpose.

I had a different experience with Coco. She died doing what she loved, and I was a part of it the entire way. Because of the way she impacted people around her with her joyful personality, I knew her purpose was served. Going out in the pursuit of your dreams was honorable despite how much it hurt.

I don't think I'll ever be able to forgive those men who were responsible for my cousins' deaths, but I had to choose not to harbor hate. I couldn't fully forgive myself with hate in my heart. The first step in learning how to forgive myself was to focus on the good in my life, the good relationships I did have and my ability in the given moment to nurture all the rest. I was now able to move differently with this new widened view. By amplifying the good, I began to drown out the feelings of hate and anger. This is what the intention of healing brought out of me. The first year of my healing journey, I realized I wasn't where I wanted to be financially, but I had a stable job with enough money that allowed me to live the lifestyle I wanted. The next step was to use this mindset to release some of the pressure off myself. I was thirty and still young. Thirty seemed to be the magic age for my generation of Black men in America. If you made it to thirty, you were lucky. If you were able to establish a sense of security by thirty, you were even luckier. But being intentional about healing also brought out the negative in me. Depression crept in and had me feeling like my luck had run out. A lot of people I know never made it to thirty; either they were dead or in jail. Obviously, there are examples of the opposite, but they weren't as prevalent throughout my life which is why the pressure to survive weighed on me so heavily. I lived some rare experiences in a short time. Will my existence escape the fate of so many like me, and will I make it into the rare breed of Black men who lived robustly into old age? Am I destined to die young? I am named after two legends whose lives were tragically cut short, after all.

I never actively thought about growing old. I never pictured myself making it to fifty. I never actively planned to survive that long. A lot of people around me were dying at young ages, so the urgency to accomplish all the things in my head was ferocious. The more "unrealistic," the more forceful the pressure. During my meditations I started to take some time to purposefully envision myself as an old man, to see and feel what that would be like. I saw myself with grandkids, still working, creating the things that I imagine. It helped me start to be kind to myself. A world of new possibilities opened for me. Look at all I accomplished in a decade starting from the bottom. I had a realization that if I have six to seven more decades to live, I could slow down. I unlocked a huge amount of mental capacity, where I had all this newfound time to make it all happen. Then I turned on the TV and saw the news that another young, unarmed Black man had been killed by police. I needed hope and I found it in my faith. I had to put all my faith in God. Not another human, system, or institution, not even in myself. God became a light that showed me hope when nothing else would. Allah saved me. Then I realized that Allah needed me as much as I needed her. It lit a new fire within me.

Battling depression wasn't easy, but fighting my way back increased my confidence in my ability to do anything I put my mind to. I had to be more honest with myself than I'd ever been before and, most importantly, I had to commit to never giving up on me. I learned the hard way that there's nothing honorable about being the cause of my own demise, especially when my loved ones were no longer able to fight for their lives. No matter how much it hurt that they weren't here anymore, I knew I had to keep moving and living. I realized in my grief that this was the only thing I owed them, but I had to think about what living looked like for me. I couldn't just exist anymore, and to move forward, I knew I had to make the conscious decision to not feel guilty about it.

LEGACY I

Whenever I thought about who I was, for the most part, it was in the frame of who I wanted to be and where I wanted to go, and not so much who or where I came from. I never had a deep connection to my family history, something I've always yearned for but didn't know how to get. After a trip to New Orleans in 2018, during my year of movement, I connected to this idea of being "my ancestors' wildest dream" after a visit to Studio BE, the art studio of emerging artist Brandan "BMike" Odums. The phrase was part of the exhibit and it reverberated throughout the entire experience. It was an immersion in this idea of legacy. I'd always wished I had a direct link to my family's roots in slavery and even pre-slavery to my African ancestry. However, decades of running from oppressive realities has removed that possibility from me. Sometimes I think the things our ancestors had to do to survive were so egregious that they made sure it remained a secret by literally taking their experiences with them to the grave. My great aunt Helen, who recently passed away, and the first and last time I'd ever met her she told me that there are certain things about my family she won't ever tell anyone. She was the last living link to the patriarch of our family heritage on my mother's side. Growing up, the story I had always been told was that both my mother's parents were adopted. I don't know much about my grandmother's family, in fact, I don't even know her maiden name. Although my grandfather was adopted, I always knew his family, which was fairly large. He had five siblings, who've created a generous number of cousins for me, but my knowledge of his family pretty much stopped there.

My quest for figuring out more of my history led me to take a road trip to Virginia to a family reunion. This was the only trip I took during my year of stillness in the summer of 2019. I drove down from NY with my mom, brother, and aunt in a rental car. I hate long-distance drives, but my family helped the time pass quickly. I thought it was important for me to go and try to gain some more knowledge about who I was and where I come from. It was there that I met my great-aunt Helen for the first time. Everyone gathered in a large hall for lunch to start the day's events. It was the perfect time for us to mingle and get to know our distant relatives. We'd spent most of the time just trying to figure out how we were all related, whipping out the family tree to get a better understanding of the lineage. It was during one of these intimate roundtable discussions that my aunt Helen revealed that my grandfather's mother, my great-grandmother, left her five kids and ran away with a cult, never to be heard from again. This was information not even my mother knew. Because my grandfather was already gone, there was no way for us to get any more details about this part of his history, to understand how he must've felt being abandoned by his mother at a young age. Aunt Helen refused to speak of my great-grandfather or where he was or anything that led to my great-grandmother's disappearance.

I couldn't understand how someone could abandon their children for a cult. I tried to understand what must've been going through her mind to do that, but it was a useless effort. Instead, I thought about what she must've gone through to get to that point. What were her parents like? What was her husband like? What was she running from? How bad was her environment that she felt she needed to leave? And am I, one of her descendants, still feeling the effects of this trauma? Is my escapism a byproduct of this generational trauma that no one ever talks about? If so, we must all be messed up. My grandfather loved his kids and grandchildren so much, I couldn't imagine how he dealt with this painful part of his past. I think about how he overcame all of that to become a chef and nutritionist at a hospital where he worked to provide a great home for his family in Harlem, even after losing everything he'd worked so hard to attain in a fire that displaced him and his entire family. It inspires me. As the victim of a house fire, he, my mom, her siblings, and my grandmother ended up in the projects. My grandfather was the only person in the household who worked; he had to start over with a family of six. He'd end up dying in those projects that helped him raise his family. As admirable as his actions were, I can never go back there. His legacy is rooted in survival, and I'm forever grateful for all that he did for our family, but his struggle won't die in vain. His legacy is us.

My family doesn't have this long legacy or direct connection to some historical feat; they're regular people who did their best to survive during a time when that was their only option. Over the past few years, I've learned a lot about my family's past. I have some hesitations even writing about it because I'm not sure if it's my story to tell, but it affected me deeply. Maybe not directly, but definitely regarding understanding who I am. When I think about my mother's side of the family, the word persistence comes to mind, moving forward through it all.

LEGACY II

My father's side of the family is large. I can link my grandmother's family pretty well from generations that are still alive, but I don't know much beyond that. I often hoped someone would take the responsibility to record and disseminate information about our history or conduct an investigation into our history beyond the past few generations. My generation, including all my cousins, takes such pride in our name and our family legacy. But what's in a name anyway? The reality is, it's a representation of who you are. Which makes me think about who we are as a family. I always come back to how my family has always done what we needed to do to survive while serving others. I remember when my grandfather, Rudolph Polite, passed away. It was the most honorable funeral service I'd ever been to. He enlisted in the U.S. Army at the age of eighteen and fought for our country, serving in Okinawa during World War II before being honorably discharged. This honor continued with a full military burial in a pristine veteran cemetery, including an honor guard detail who presented my father with an American flag in his honor. It was that moment when I doubled down on my authority as an American citizen and the rights afforded to me. We are America, and I decided then that I'd do my best to make sure no one can take it from us. I saw that the culmination of my grandfather's life was relegated to family and service. I couldn't think of a better legacy to leave in the end, a legacy rooted in what you've done for others. It has nothing to do with a name, bank account, or any material things.

One of the last acts of survival that my grandfather committed practically erased the generational wealth he worked his entire life to build and maintain. On the outside, it would seem as though this was his legacy: a multi-family house in Queens on a corner lot that served as the Polite residence for more than fifty years. The house was hanging on by a thread due to low maintenance throughout the years, but it served as a central meeting ground for the entire family. My grandfather had paid his house off decades ago, so he lived out the later years of his life with no mortgage but with a number of his children and their family members who still lived with him. It also served as a place for any of his grandchildren to come to stay whenever they needed time to get back on their feet.

After my grandmother passed away, and with what I'm sure had to be mounting bills, he made a decision to help him survive the last few years of his life. After being approached by predatory lenders, he entered into a reverse mortgage contract. He didn't seek advice from anyone, he just did what he had always done: whatever he needed to survive. This contract that he signed offered him $80,000 without any obligation to pay it back. But at the time of his death, if the family could not purchase the mortgage back, this company would gain control of the house. Now, $80,000 might not seem like much and surely my family, with his remaining nine children, could have come up with the necessary funds. What these lenders didn't tell my grandfather was that they had the right to sell his contract to another lender for market price. By the time my grandfather passed away, the contract had been sold so many times, in a matter of two years the price went from $80,000 to $450,000, rendering it nearly impossible for any of my family members to be able to take on that kind of investment. At first, the family was upset by this; the home they grew up in, which they thought would be theirs, was now gone. I think about all the different ways this could have played out. If my grandfather was open enough to come to the family for help before making that kind of decision or if the family had done a better job of helping him maintain the house over the years, it might have been a different story. My grandfather's last wish wasn't to continue to provide for his grown children. He wished to survive in the best way he could. No one can fault him for that. He was trapped inside the survival mentality like so many of us, and when his back was against the wall, he did what he felt was the best thing for him.

Losing that house caused me to think about my identity in relation to it. Like a lot of things life has thrown at me, I never imagined that house belonging to anyone outside my family. It's been a part of my life from the day I was born. I didn't live there, but it always served as a reprieve for me. I would leave the projects of East Harlem to travel to Ozone Park, Queens, New York. It was such a different life than the one I lived on a daily basis. I loved spending long weeks there during the summer. I woke up every morning to breakfast my grandmother cooked for all her grandchildren, who'd also be there. I spent time with my cousins developing those deep bonds that only cousins could. The main feelings that come to mind from the time I spent at my second home are sentimentality and nostalgia. There's no price that could equal the value of that, but there's certainly a price set by the market that puts a monetary value on the property.

Sentimentality and nostalgia are two principles that can cause us to hold on to things longer than necessary, whether it's real estate, valuables, or relationships. These principles caused me to try and do everything I could to save my grandparents' house, even though I knew it would be a bad investment. Now, I wonder when this emotional response began within the human evolutionary framework, because from my experience it seems like a direct contradiction to life's ever-changing reality. In this framework, struggle and pain are caused by an inability to let go, move forward, and thrive in a new reality. As humans, we relate these things to who we are, our identity, so letting go can feel like we're abandoning a part of ourselves. To grow and thrive, we have to make room for new things and relationships to define who we are in our current state. I've come to identify myself based on the long line of survivors with a legacy of service to others. That's what occupies my family history. And that's a good enough high-level perspective for me as I try to move forward in my life with those same intentions while evolving from survival mode to thrive mode. In my current reality, I'm identifying myself on a granular level as an author, entrepreneur, son, brother, cousin, friend, godfather, etc. My idea of thriving is being my best at every part of me during their respective times. This is why I've gained a minimalist mindset, so I don't get attached to too many material things that don't relate to my identity or purpose. The more I think about what it would mean to thrive, I understand that by making it OK for myself to thrive, I make it OK for those around me to do the same. From the outside, my late grandfather's decision to choose his survival seemed selfish at first. But I believe that it was his last great act of kindness to his children, forcing them to evolve by removing their safety net. He did his job and provided until his last breath. He fulfilled his purpose. I can't imagine it was an easy decision to make. Sometimes, what's necessary is the hardest.

LEGACY PREP

Throughout my journey, I never thought about the lessons I was gaining about what I would like to pass down to my children. Having my own family was never something I aspired to. I figured I'd have one eventually, but it was never a goal that I actively worked toward achieving until now. I had to get myself mentally ready first. I'd been scarred from seeing so many people have kids at young ages before they were fully prepared to take on the responsibility of an additional mind or before they had the chance to heal from their trauma and develop their own mind, thus advancing the beast that is generational trauma. They often didn't even realize that they were doing it. I wanted to end that cycle with myself and raise mentally healthy children. Growing up in the projects, I saw how mentally unhealthy our community could be. I saw people make decisions about their lives that just didn't seem normal, and yet in our world it was. But I didn't know any better. Venturing outside of the only box I knew helped me learn how healthy minds operated. Exposure and experience were key in being able to recognize my own issues. Part of what kept me alive during my dark times was fully coming to grips with my capabilities, not for what I can do for myself but for others, including a future family. Finding this sense of purpose helped me get here.

Prioritizing having a family of my own helped me get into an adult mindset. I want to be a husband and a dad. I find nobility in those titles. I realized that by running away from those things, I was pushing off my responsibility of continuing our legacy. I was afraid of what those responsibilities would mean for my reality. I was on a mission to figure out how to positively change the world, but facing the hurt I felt every time the world proved a disappointment caused my desire to help to decrease significantly. I was afraid of what that meant for me going forward. I knew it would mean a drastic change in my lifestyle, in my values and beliefs in what I've known to be right. And besides, I was still developing my mind and figuring new things out about myself and the world around me. I equated starting a family with the loss of that ability.

One of my main goals now is to build a loving family that

is able to live a long and prosperous life filled with purpose and service. I knew, though, that I couldn't achieve this goal until I lived it myself. I had to find a way to live my life in purpose and service so that I could be the example for my future children, the way my dad was for me. I had to continue the growth of our legacy, God willing, of course. I needed to really imagine myself as a dad and husband. What would that look and feel like? I never pictured it until after I embarked on this healing journey. The answers I came up with helped keep me motivated. They helped me make the conscious decision to pursue celibacy for the duration of my healing journey.

I realized how much of my energy I was giving to women who weren't the one for me. It was my ego that led me down a path that I didn't want. I had to get control. I had to be disciplined enough to know that it would be worth it in the end. I knew that recharging and keeping my energy stored away for the love of my life would be the best thing I could do in the present moment for my future family. I just had to focus on getting myself right so that when our paths crossed, I would be ready. I understand my humanity better, and I know I'm flawed like the rest of us. There were many times when I almost gave in to temptation, but I thank Allah that she was able to keep me on this path. It was something that became important for me to see through. It was one of my biggest challenges after spending years letting my insecurities dictate my love life. I now found myself wanting to pursue love from a place of strength. This newfound understanding of energy, spirituality, and the infinity of the universe that I gained during this healing journey left me not wanting to give my energy to infinite women, but to give infinite energy to one woman who could reciprocate. I wanted a partner I could live with in every dimension. I felt secure in this vision.

My parents are still together and happily married, which is rare these days. It's actually been rare my entire life. Growing up, my parents were the only couple I knew who were married. Until I was in my twenties, theirs was the only wedding I'd ever been to. I've watched them as they've gone on this journey of life together; through all its ups and downs, they've balanced each other out. I admire them a lot because they've been through so much and still maintain the strength to keep working at building the life they envision for themselves. They're flawed just like the rest of us but they never gave up on each other. As part of my healing process, I had to remove the parental lens that I'd always worn so I could see them as humans. It was an eye-opening experience for me. I retold myself stories from our past and placed myself in their shoes. They were always my superheroes, even when we fought. I now see them as superhumans, who raised more superhumans.

I'd often focus on the struggle of building a life with someone, rather than the benefits that could come from it. I think it's because negativity played such a huge part in the everyday grind of my environment. It was the struggle that I was running away from whenever I subconsciously, or consciously, sabotaged one of my relationships. Coming to terms with the fact that life will always be a struggle at every stage and that it just takes a different form, helped me to make the goal of starting a family a priority. Finding a wife now looks like finding someone I feel comfortable being in the trenches with. As a man, I still want to be secure enough to provide but I'm secure enough in myself now to know that no matter what happens, I will always find a way to safety because I am a product of survival. It's in my genes, a legacy that has been passed down to me, even though I now see and accept my responsibility to evolve our legacy. I believe that's part of my purpose. I'd like for the next generations to be able to pinpoint the time when their ancestors began to thrive in society. It's already started and I only hope to continue to do whatever is necessary to advance our evolution.

To My Unborn Child:

You don't even exist, and yet you saved me. When I thought about loving you, I felt my heart beat again. I hadn't for a while. My heart was broken and no matter how much I tried to heal it, it just couldn't get completely whole. Thinking about you made my heart feel whole again. If I'm being honest, I'm not sure it's ever felt like this. The possibility of this kind of love is new territory for me. I immediately knew that I was always going to do what's best for you. I promise to be the best dad I can be. My goal is to create the perfect balance between discipline and freedom to help you become your best self. I'll make some mistakes, I'm sure of it. It's human nature. One thing I can promise is that I'll never give up on you. I'll never give up on us. I don't know what stage of life I'll be in when you arrive, if you ever arrive, whether I'm poor or wealthy, my dreams fulfilled or unfulfilled. But I know that you will become my first priority, always. Glory always comes after struggle.

To My Future Wife:

I don't know when our paths will cross, or if they've crossed already. But what I do know is that I'd take my commitment to you very seriously. When I dream of the perfect life together I don't dream of fancy cars and designer clothes. I dream of peace, joy, and security. I dream of a foundation built on God. I dream of our union being guided by faith. I dream of a 'what's best for us?' mindset. Radical love will be our superpower. It'll have rippling effects for generations. I can't wait to hear your vision for us. I hope I can be the man you're able to trust forever.

THE SUN AND THE MOON

I love the sun. The beach is my favorite place to be. I love lying on dense sand, kneading a handful of grains, feeling each one slip through my fingers as I soak up the sun's rays—and repeat. There's a rejuvenating energy I get from it. I always feel refreshed after a beach vacation and ready to continue my journey. I've scoured the earth for spots where I feel closest to the sun, where I could get a glimpse of the beauty of sunrises and sunsets from every coast in North America to Greek Islands, Japanese mountaintops, African deserts, from the Caribbean to South America, and a multitude of spots in between. The sun always served me by illuminating my aura and reminding me of my power. Until recently, I never felt that much of a connection with the moon. My year of stillness was the first year I didn't chase the sun. I spent a couple of hours in Virginia Beach during my family reunion, but other than that, nothing.

During that fall and winter, when I moved to upstate New York to live with my parents, I got the opportunity to get reacquainted with the moon. Not living in the city opened up the sky for me. I would often sit in the woods at night looking up at the moon, soaking in its rays. There was a magnetic energy that I bonded with, one that was rejuvenating, but in a way that sparked my creativity. It was a grounding energy that helped me look deeper inside myself. I was at a low point during this time in my life and I realized that the moon provided light in my darkness in the form of writing, which helped bring me clarity. The darkness that was inside me needed to connect to moonlight. Part of healing meant using that moonlight to guide me out of the darkness I was stuck in so I could connect to my sunlight, bask in the shine of my aura, and illuminate the good in my life. The darkness got heaviest when I couldn't find appreciation for the light. There was the moon reminding me that light is always within me, even in darkness. It was a constant reminder that the sun always sets. When it does, all I need to do is find my moonlight and patiently wait until the sun returns to illuminate my aura. The sun and the moon became the physical representations of the ups and downs of my life. There's beauty in both. I've learned to live happily through it all.

"Just because a man lacks the use of his eyes doesn't mean he lacks vision."

- Stevie Wonder

PART 3:

THRIVE, BY ANY MEANS NECESSARY

BULLETPROOF

The healing process was all worth it. The solitude, the failed relationships, the brutal honesty, it all led to more vibrant and beautiful relationships. I see the change in me in real time. With my mind in a better place, I knew it was time to focus on my financial health. I've learned that at the heart of capitalism lies long-term planning and growth. And I wanted to adopt that mentality in regards to creating generational wealth. When it comes to creating generational wealth for Black Americans as a whole it often feels like we're constantly playing catch-up making it hard to ever truly get ahead. It's how our wealth generating system is designed. I believe that until Black people come together to create and stick to a unified agenda that benefits us then we'll continue to play catch up. In our "democracy," a unified agenda leads to long-term wealth and prosperity. It's no secret that white men control a majority of the wealth in this country. The structure of wealth distribution in today's business world still resembles this methodology. For example, most of the venture capital designated to push the country forward goes to white men, distributed for the most part by other white men. I sat in on a panel where I heard a white man talk about getting $160 million for his start-up idea. He boasted about failing, then going back to successfully raise an additional $90 million because he was now more experienced. Black people rarely, if ever, get these kinds of opportunities. We must be perfectly scrappy for scraps.

How could we see this opportunity within ourselves if we never see anyone who looks like us with these kinds of stories? Access to capital is access to stories and stories shape perception.

I've found that by consciously changing my perception about who I am, where I come from, and who my people are to view us as beings who operate at the highest levels of greatness, I bring myself closer to God. It allows me to live in that frequency I unlock when I meditate. Every time I work on an aspect of myself, I feel like I'm building myself in God's image. So how could I not believe that Black men and women aren't the chosen ones? I realized that if I couldn't see God in others who looked like me, how could I ever see her within me?

Money has become a tool to be used like a gun. We were out-armed when they took us as slaves and now, we're out-capitalized. We can't thrive without power, and I often thought I needed capital for power until I realized that God is power and once we tap into our power, an abundance of capital and tools we need to thrive will flow to us.

During my year of stillness, I let go of worrying about money, and it allowed me the freedom to paint whatever picture I wanted. It was important for me to paint a picture of truth. Some of the greatest hoaxes of all time continue to be the redistribution of images of Black terror through media propaganda as well as an education curriculum that's been set by white people; required textbooks are the definition of revisionist history, written to appease rather than educate on truth. This system continues to dictate how we see ourselves and what we can and cannot learn while making higher education out of reach for minorities and the poor. Misinformation has become a bullet that kills critical thinking, self-worth, and pride. Capitalism is the gun that fires that bullet, allowing it to reach as many of us as possible. Taking the time to educate myself about myself has given me the confidence to stand firm in the highest regard of my being, making me bulletproof.

DAMAGE CONTROL

The concept of Diversity Equity, and Inclusion (DEI) should look like a myriad of cultures and backgrounds coming together to make decisions that will affect the overall population of whatever community it's serving, not just a select few from similar backgrounds. When it comes to our political landscape, for example, a lack of diversity will always produce one-sided agendas. Too often the stories our politicians, majority white males, tell themselves promote oppressive laws as a survival strategy. These strategies, which tend to concentrate power to a singular group, can't be peacefully sustained, especially not in one as large as U.S. history. As history will tell us, it leads to war and terror. But in the U.S. war and terror creates wealth for white men. The fact of the matter is the U.S. is very diverse and the decisions about our future need to be as well for peace and prosperity. We must demand just, moral, and intelligent leaders, leaving no room for corruption or selfishness amongst "leaders of the free world," our world. It's free because we say so. We can't let certain individuals destroy our civil liberties or our rights as humans.

Topics such as DEI have become more political buzzwords than a cultural necessity so that the appearance and perception of its existence are more important than living and breathing its essence. Organizations have used DEI to elevate their social status (insert press release here) to boost their reputation and their profits. DEI has become damage control, but the minority groups it's meant to uplift are more than that. It's also become weaponized against Black and Brown people by white women coopting the movement. The interconnectedness between DEI and feminism is complicated. Both movements are important. But when white women become the face of DEI they tend to drown out the voices of other minority groups including women of color. This became extremely apparent to me when I sat in on a DEI panel at Stanford GSB where the undertone of the entire talk was directed toward women in the workplace, with barely any specific mention of women of color, queer women, or any other minority group.

During my year of movement, I flew to San Francisco to attend my yearly Ignite reunion. It was my first time on campus, three years after the completion of my program which took place in New York. The main campus in Palo Alto was everything I imagined it to be. I was surrounded by excellence again. There were a host of events planned for the weekend, and I was eager to dive in and begin networking. The reunion was for Ignite alumni from all cohorts across the globe as well as MBA alumni. I met a myriad of brilliant people who were passionately working on solutions for a multitude of problems from trying to end poverty and fighting addiction through awareness to building commercial grade 3D-printed airplanes. The conversations were never dull. Those were just some examples of the Black excellence that I was surrounded by. We were outnumbered by far, but the impact that radiated was immense. It was the fuel that I needed. It also opened my eyes to the amount of work that was still necessary.

One of the weekend events included a panel on DEI. It was moderated by the dean of the business school, who'd been recently appointed to the position. I was excited about this panel because we were at one of the most progressive business schools in the world and this was a topic that was near and dear to my heart. I was eager to hear the view from the top on this subject. Yet, I ended up extremely disappointed again. The panel included the first woman faculty member at the GSB, who had completed her last lecture earlier that same day, and the head of DEI at the GSB. In total, the panel consisted of a white male and two white women. It was spring 2018, and this was not the image of DEI I was expecting to see. However, it did mirror what I'd been seeing throughout the country. I was still excited about the talk though; surely, there was a lot to talk about on the subject. I was wrong again. The DEI in this talk was relegated to only one thing: work/life balance for women in the workplace. While this is an important topic of DEI, whose importance and value for inclusion work can't be overlooked, the talk was very one-sided, exclusionary even, and seemed to miss the mark completely. When it comes to these discussions, I think context matters. If we're going to talk diversity and inclusion we must represent diverse groups and be nuanced about the many differences each group may face.

In today's society women still experience gender oppression and discrimination, and we can't take away from their struggle in their fight for equality. We're all in this together. However, there must come a point when white women must acknowledge that they benefit from discriminatory practices through the privileges they indirectly receive from their white male counterparts, be it their fathers, husbands, or sons. They must hold them accountable in a way only they can. My biggest concern was that during the talk, there was no mention of the differences in the plight for women of color. There was no mention of any other minority group at all. Issues such as the pay gap for women is very different for women of color whose gap much wider than white womens. The number of women of color on corporate boards or in C-suites is dismal in comparison to white women. We can't run from these differences, we have to face them head on to make change.

As a Black man, I can personally attest to the daily fight against discrimination in the workplace. There are many ways DEI can help build a better world. For me, it was disheartening to sit there and listen to this panel boil it down to having a work-life balance for women. To be a true DEI champion, any conversation, panel, team, or organization in America that promotes or claims to engage in any form of diversity initiative must have a Black person involved at the highest level. Period. Otherwise, are you diverse and inclusive?

I believe it is important for us to call out white women who fail to recognize their own privilege as they fight for justice, especially if they have a large platform. Time was limited during this panel, but the three individuals who were speaking had enough clout and power for their voices to be heard and felt as a standard. And they were speaking to our country's current and future leaders who'd then go off into their respective corners of the world and make decisions based on what they'd heard. I have high standards though, and their talk was echoing the oppression of minority groups of color through blatant omission, which didn't even come close to meeting my standards. I think this stuck out to me so much because it mirrored what I'd been seeing in the media and real life, where the white feminism movement is just simply out of touch with the rest of the world. I'm afraid that this trend, if not checked, can reframe the image of what DEI truly looks like: white women unintentionally, or intentionally, further oppressing other marginalized groups while advancing the agenda of their white male counterparts, an opinion that I established way before sitting in on this panel discussion. It was a defining moment for me that reinforced the need for minority groups to not only be visible in these spaces so that our voices can be heard but also to continue to do the work ourselves to advance our own agenda so we can thrive. I realized then that I couldn't sit back and wait for things to change nor expect others to fight for people that look like me, at least not on a large scale. It's up to us to demand justice and protect our progress. Don't get me wrong, I don't believe there was any malicious intent during this panel. I do believe though that our nation's most sacred and prized organizations should be more cognizant of how they present certain issues to the world. It's not that hard, and I don't think understanding this perspective is too much to ask from some of the world's greatest minds. If it is, that means it'll be a futile act trying to get the rest of the world to understand, which should scare us into doing the work to make it easier for others to internalize. We can thrive as a society, together.

NEXT GEN

We live in a society in which we're constantly dehumanizing each other which causes us to dehumanize ourselves. We're being the biggest hypocrites. We tell each other not to feel, even though we know we feel. We say take emotion out of business, but how is that humanly possible? Being in the technology and business industries, I often think about what the next generation of great products will look like. My newfound clarity leads me to believe that the best products are going to be those made with emotion, for our emotions. We want our products to be convenient to help make our lives a little easier. We will soon want our products to not just know us but know how we feel. We'll want our experiences to be tailored and personal because it makes us feel special. We can't build these products if we're devoid of emotion, if we aren't at least self-aware. This doesn't mean dismissing analytics from our methodologies. We live in a data-first world, and our decision-making skills should encompass both our Emotional Intelligence (EQ) and IQ. For Black people to thrive in this technological revolution we must utilize both. I believe we're already ahead of the game when it comes to EQ; it's evident in our culture. We have the power to create a world that benefits us instead of one that suppresses our magic. We're extremely intelligent already. We must continue to further our education in all fields.

FREEDOM

I used to think freedom was about my ability to do whatever I wanted. I had to face the fact that that's going to be impossible. I'm starting to become OK with knowing that not everything is meant for me. What's meant for me will come to me, no matter how long the journey. My peace with this comes from my new understanding of freedom. The freedom to be 100 percent me along the way. Understanding that my self-awareness, and the confidence that comes with it, is a superpower helped me to unleash this kind of freedom. When I started to think about how I've been able to survive in many different environments, it came down to my ability to code-switch and adapt to any situation that arose. Whether it's dealing with gangsters in the street, or sharks in the boardroom. It's a skill that I've developed over time without even knowing it. It helped build my ability to compartmentalize, which is another superpower when used with self-awareness. For a long time, I thought that was a negative characteristic. I thought it meant I didn't really belong anywhere. Instead of running from it, I decided to embrace it and use it to my advantage by changing my perspective on how I viewed code-switching, not as a burden or a mask I had to put on and take off during designated times but a tool or a utility to help me navigate the world where everyone was different. I think there's a strong correlation between the freedom to show up in spaces as your full self and code-switching. I realized the switch was just a part of me that I decided to amplify at any given moment. I recognized the power behind the active control and management of how I decide to show up. It didn't make me any less of myself. I just figured out how to be me within the context of my environment. I can go with the vibe or set my own when given the opportunity; that's my magic. What good is having magical powers if you aren't going to use them? Most Black professionals understand this concept and how to harness it to excel in their respective spaces. It's part of our cultural identity and should be documented in history as such.

I believe we all have the freedom to be great in our own ways, but if there's anything my year of stillness taught me, it's that greatness is high-maintenance. If you're not actively seeking it out and cultivating it, it will leave you. I believe that no matter where my personal pursuits of greatness take me, I'm grateful for the freedom to pursue it. That gratitude made me realize that if I wasn't actively embracing my role and responsibility as a human being living on this planet, then I could never truly embody greatness. If there was no love in me, then I definitely couldn't reach my potential greatness. Love is hard and hate is too easy. I recognized that the purity of my greatness would lie within the intent of my actions, not the outcome.

Vulnerability has been the price I've had to pay for the privilege of pursuing purpose. I had to allow myself to be open so that I could be available to receive the blessings I needed to continue in my pursuits. This realization was extremely difficult for me to internalize. It went against a lifetime of conditioning that taught me that men weren't vulnerable. Instead, we bottled up our feelings and emotions and tucked them deep inside ourselves. Confronting my true feelings face-to-face was one of the most difficult things for me to do, but it has also been one of the most liberating.

It was very difficult for me to come to the realization that the pursuit of perfection was a frivolous act. Being no. 1 in something is great, whether you're the no. 1 draft pick or you're at top of your class at the best school in the world. Those things are great, but it took getting no. 1 spots to realize that it wasn't greatness that I'd achieved. I now see that even in the face of the best accolades, when I strive to match that same energy in my pursuit to be the best human I can be, only then can I embody greatness: the best son, dad, partner, friend, cousin, brother, etc. that I can be. That's how I want to thrive in this world. A lot of Black men don't get the opportunity to show up in this way. These opportunitties are often stipped from us, whether by the criminal justice system, economic injustice, mental health crisis, etc. This is why thriving in freedom to me means being able to find purpose in helping others.

BASIC INSTINCT x DESIGN THINKING

I was the first in my family to go away to a four-year college which meant that I didn't have much prior knowledge about the journey I'd chosen to embark on. I was hungry and I followed my instincts, the only thing I had. These instincts helped me survive growing up in the hood and often led me to succeed in my various academic, extracurricular, and professional pursuits. Over time, my confidence grew. What I've realized about instincts is that sometimes they're right and sometimes they're wrong. When I gravitated toward the things I was instinctively right about, I found success. But when I either ignored my instinct or gravitated toward something I felt was instinctively wrong, I found disappointment. Both cases usually created ripple effects. As part of my healing process, I had to get back in tune with my instincts so that I could tap into my supreme confidence again, the innate belief in myself that had gotten me this far. When my world got turned upside down, I found myself in new territory, and it was hard to trust my instincts, especially because I was getting older and now had so much to lose. I started to second-guess myself and it caused me to have a debilitating anxiety. Goal setting helped me overcome this. Whenever I wound up in turbulent times, I referred to my road map to help ground me, a road map that I designed for myself based on the instincts that often led me to success.

Design Thinking is a concept that I learned about at Stanford. It's a concept that was built upon with the creation of the design school to help entrepreneurs and organizations map their customer journey to help them create the best possible product. The idea of using design theory as a scientific approach to solving complex issues started in the 1960's. It's definied as a non-linear, iterative process that teams use to understand users, challenge assumptions, redefine problems and create innovative solutions to prototype and test. Involving five phases—Empathize,

Define, Ideate, Prototype and Test—it is most useful to tackle problems that are ill-defined or unknown.

After years of studying how organizations designed great products, I figured I could use this design-thinking process to design my greatest life. To empathize with myself so I can uncover my problem areas, define them, then ideate on solutions to those problems. Then prototype and test my theories. I amended the design-thinking proccess to focus on my personal journeys and goals. I was the user, and life was the product. This excersise was extremely helpful in uncovering the conditioning and trauma that was holding me back from living my greatest life. It helped me figure out how to find my purpose. With so many benefits, I knew I needed to bring this to more people. I decided to facilitate a design-thinking workshop called The New Normal with a group of Black men in order to test its impact on the goals of other Black men. I'd found that using design thinking to create my story helped me gain a clear understanding of my goals while crafting a strategy with action items to help get me there and it might be able to help others.

My theory was that this way of thinking could help advance Black men by removing the ideas the world had about us and craft our ideal lives. Too often we're expected to just know without any resources or support. So, I wanted to create that, at least for those in my circle that I could reach. Doing this in a group setting proved even more helpful. Participants gained perspective and ideas from others that they may have never thought about alone. I'd reached out to about twenty-five men and found eight willing and able to participate. Our group came from all different professional backgrounds and their goals ranged from creating generational wealth or getting a job after graduation to running a marathon. I'd invited the group to my office on a Saturday when I knew no one would be in. At the time, I was working in Times Square in a modern open-concept office, which made the setting perfect for collaboration and inspiring ideas. I paired everyone up with a partner for the first half of the workshop and then we ended with a group brainstorming session to pool our resources and ideas to help each other reach our goals. It reaffirmed to me how much we could thrive when we worked together. It was a blueprint for our advancement. We have so many images and stories about how Black men don't work together or how we're always against each other. For us to thrive, we have to categorically reject this notion. There was so much success that came from this workshop, but others stories are not mine to tell.

There were so many times along my journey when I was forced to think outside the box to survive. I decided it was easier just to live outside the box. Make it a lifestyle and I'd always find my way, I thought. I've always been goal oriented, doing whatever it took to accomplish my goals. When I began using Design Thinking to construct my ideal lifestyle, I felt healed by the possibilities. I realized early on in my journey that there was no room for normal in-the-box thinking because there will always be problems. I thought living outside the box was the mindset to have, but I was just leaving one box for another. Maybe it was a little easier to live and survive in, but it wasn't my box. It wasn't until I surrendered to my creativity that I found the ability to design the box of my dreams, with infinite options for how I could thrive within it.

BLACK REVOLUTIONS

There's a quote by Dr. Martin Luther King Jr., "There comes a time when silence is betrayal." For so long that quote was one-dimensional for me. I thought it meant I had to speak up about the things that were happening to my people. It's why developed a passion for telling our stories, and one of the reasons I co-founded my media company, Black Bravado. I couldn't stay silent about what it looks like on the other side of struggle. My cousin Shakira and I got the idea for Black

Bravado after struggling to deal with the unjust killing of young Michael Brown at the hands of the police in Ferguson, Missouri. Tired of seeing images of Black death we wanted to create a platform to showcase what we saw in us; the positivity, the love, the excellence in all fields. This became our contribution to the movement. We saw massive success in our early years, because what we were doing was desperately needed in our community. Uplifting while the world tried to oppress us.

I came across the MLK quote again while embarking on my healing journey and it took on an entirely new meaning for me. I realized I couldn't be silent about my story. In doing so, I was betraying myself, and that wasn't love. We speak up for love. Love inspired this poem.

"One After Another"
I Love Black People the way I Love Freedom.
I Pray for Freedom for All of Us.
How do we Escape?
How do we Build?
How do we Thrive?
Fight by Fight
Brick by Brick
One After Another.

Allah has become my center. I wouldn't be here without him. It was easy for me to accept Allah once I realized my God was Black. In what I think was one of my most revolutionary acts, I gave him a face that resembled mine. With that, I found a comfort in worship that I'd never felt before. If all my idols are Black, why shouldn't my God be? That was the disconnect in my faith. For as long as I could remember I'd been shown images of God as a white man on a cross. I could identify with the nobility in theory, but I never connected with the image. Once I gave myself permission to see Allah in an image I could relate to, it was easier for me to strengthen my faith. It became easier for me to see Black people for who we really are and easier to see myself for who I really am, a child of Allah.

During the darkest times of my depression, I pleaded with Allah for clear skies. I felt I'd proved I could weather any storm. I was convinced that I'd earned a smooth sail. After changing my idea of who God was, he responded by revealing my power to control my weather and reminded me that I always had that power. I just had to become fully aware of it. I'd tapped into it to survive, but I didn't know how to tap into it to thrive. Talking with him helped me realize that every human on earth has this God-given power and, as individuals, this is the power we should be fighting for. Oppressors don't want us to realize this. They prefer us unaware to make it easier for them to control us. I often interchanged power and influence in a way that made power seem out of reach. Power over myself felt more effective than power over other people ever did. Once I realized this, I saw how my presence affected people. This power I had over myself created influence. That's what I'm inspired by now, people who can control their weather and people who've made it through the storm and lived to tell their stories. There are so many of us.

Every day more and more Black people are coming out of the storm and realizing their strength. We are shifting culture to represent our time to thrive in modern society. There's no doubt that individuals, organizations, and systems continue to actively try to oppress us. They're only making us stronger. The adversity we face creates a resourcefulness that can never be taught. Forced to be creative, we're flipping the table over, using our culture to improve our world, and we're doing it with ownership. We are the future, and our efforts need to be supported, especially those of young people, of all races, who are leading the charge for change. We face new challenges that need new, fresh solutions, and to thrive we need to include young people in the conversation for change. Older generations tend to be experienced in solving the problems of their generation, but they haven't had to take into consideration new threats, like the urgency of climate change. If we are to innovate and evolve together, we can't clamp on to old ideals that clearly don't work in the modern world. We can't deny science, we must lean into it. There's no time to fight each other when we have to save the planet. Given the rapid change of technology, I believe we can create an environment for not only our generation but future generations as well to thrive. In every generation, there are people who believe they are superior, that their way is the best and only way. There are also those that are interested in amassing power but for their own benefit. Power should be used to do good for others. Once we have it, we need to use it to help others who look like us. That's how we can thrive collectively and constantly. Power is fleeting, but we can pass it down before we lose it. That's why I try to aim less for power and more for influence. What's the point of having power if it's self-serving? That's wasted power. Power comes with a responsibility to use it as a progressive tool, especially since the power of the people is a force that can never be reckoned with. It has toppled regimes many times before. The tribal instincts of human nature tell us if there are oppressors, there will always be revolutionaries. Black people power the revolutions.

ONLY THE WEALTHY SURVIVE

Darwinism is a theory that our strength determines our survival. We've normalized the strong eating the weak, but I believe in radically changing this perspective. I believe the strong should compassionately and vigorously protect the weak. Human nature is complex. With elements like the ego, which is often self-serving. Without it though, I question if humans would have had the innovations that helped advance our society. It takes ego to believe in a vision enough to pursue it. What I've learned is that like everything else, ego is a skill that can be managed and harnessed for good. If we are to thrive as a people, we need to find the ego balance that allows us to believe in ourselves as individuals without losing empathy for the community as a whole. Individualism tells us that the idea of survival of the fittest should be foundational. But the strongest foundations that are built to last are created and upheld by the community in which the individual is born from.

In the capitalist society that we live in, strength is often defined by net worth, expanding the ego of the wealthy while diminishing the ego of the poor. If we think our worth and ideas aren't valuable because we're poor, we're leaving our advancement as humans on the table; this is a huge barrier to Black people's ability to thrive given the extreme wealth inequality we're experiencing. When the ego is fueled, we innovate. We feel empowered to find a solution to a problem that we've recognized. But the thing about innovation today is: only the wealthy survive. This is why I've become an advocate for Black people taking wealth building seriously. For too long, we've been left out of considerations for economic advancement in a world that constantly takes from us, whether it's our lives, our labor, or our ideas that often generate wealth for others. Yet, still, we consume before we save. We engage in fratricidal rivalries over who has more, even if more is only a small fraction. We view life insurance as a scam or superfluous, when a small monthly payment can make sure our kids and their kids struggle a little less after we're gone. We can afford a legacy if we prioritize it. We can afford to survive, but we have to fight for it.

UNIVERSAL LANGUAGE

I think about the English language and how someone had to create it. Someone had to define it. Someone created a language that billions of people would learn and use as a tool for communication. They convinced the world that it was in their best interest to speak English. They made it the language of the world, a legacy that would benefit their own forever.

This is a product of ego. In every foreign country I've visited, I found natives who spoke English. Knowing English typically gave them an edge in a job market created around tourism and created the illusion of advancement as a reward for learning English. This capitalized on the ego of the individual, using imaginary currency to finance investments in infrastructure that literally paved the road for such advancements. The American passport has become one of the most respected documents of identification and allows US citizens to maneuver almost effortlessly across the globe, boosting the economy of other nations through tourism and creating leverage out of experience.

The same thing is happening with the technological revolution. The technological creators are the ones who will control the world for generations to come. They could create new universal languages. They have the power and influence to force the world to adopt their language by convincing consumers that it's in their best interest to use their products, creating leverage by offering convenience and accessibility in exchange for their data. This commodity has become more valuable than oil. Think Google, Apple, or Amazon. We are speaking their language. I aim to be a voice that speaks up on the fact that we, as Black people, could create our own language. Blindly adopting the language of others only enables us to live in their world with no choice but to play by their rules. To thrive, we have to create more and consume less.

THRIVING WITH MENTAL HEALTH ISSUES

When I first found out that Dr. Martin Luther King Jr. and Malcolm X suffered from mental health issues such as depression and alleged schizophrenia, I knew I was in good company. But I wanted to understand why. One of the things I've come to understand is that there was a real link to associating mental disorders with African Americans during the civil rights movement. Advertisements and propaganda regarding the disease flooded the market with African images. It was another example of using the media to further oppress Black people. It's the negative connotation that came with it that forced Black people to reject the notion of it altogether, so as not to get sucked into the narrative. I think it's why we struggle today to come to terms with mental health issues. At a time when the media was telling us we were crazy and forcing medicine on us, we had to fight back against it, even if we did have mental health issues. When Malcolm X was diagnosed with schizophrenia because of his alleged paranoia about the government coming after him, the media made him out to be crazy when, in fact, he was right. Can you blame Black men for being wary of seeking help and having someone diagnose us with any kind of mental health issues? It's no wonder our first inclination is to dismiss it altogether.

MLK Jr. suffered from depression and refused to seek help for it. After doing some quick research, this illness kept popping up for individuals like him who are driven by purpose; depression is common and not necessarily a bad thing. It's the direct effect of being a leader who's able to empathize with society in order to come up with creative solutions. These skills are reserved for some of the best leaders of our time. The sentiment is that dealing with depression is tolerable in the face of the greater good. As we evolve and learn from each other, we learn how to adjust. What I've learned is that sacrificing yourself for the sake of sacrifice isn't honorable as much as it is misguided. I believe leaders who partake in social sciences can take care of themselves while embracing the needs of the world. The best leaders can use empathy to discern what cause they're compelled to embrace. By approaching every human interaction with an empathetic mindset, the authenticity and sincerity of the exchange become heightened. The connection you make can then result in either "I understand," or "I'm trying to understand." If it's neither, then you can gracefully exit the situation. It's not for you and that's OK too. To thrive as leaders, we have to seek help when we need it. I was so reluctant to seek help until my burden became too heavy to bear on my own. I wish I'd received help sooner, but I use my testimony as a cautionary tale and a reframing and normalization of Black men seeking help and care when their mind is sick.

LEADERSHIP

There are many definitions of leadership. I've studied leadership for over a decade and, to me, it's the ability to know and trust yourself enough to spark movement within a group by enlisting a majority in your vision to improve or create a path toward a common goal. Leaders are visionaries who master the balance of risk and caution to do whatever it takes to make their visions a reality, visions that are so clear they seem like reality before execution. Leaders are willing to take certain risks because, with those kinds of visions, sometimes it's more of a risk to not do everything in your power to make them come to life. It's not uncommon for true leaders to be haunted by the path they're called to embark on. Especially when the stakes in direct proportion to the potential impact on others are high. I've often found myself haunted by my visions, constantly nagging at me and forcing me to get up and act. This is one of the reasons I had to learn how to lead myself before I could step into a true leadership role. I couldn't rely on my visions themselves anymore. More importantly, I realized it's where the lessons were. I'd succumbed to this widening gap between my visions and my execution of them. I had a lack of understanding or transparency of the sacrifices and effort it was going to take from me to make my visions come true, and I knew this gap could only be narrowed by knowledge of myself. It helped me conclude that leadership is the process of identifying and narrowing that gap for myself and others so that we could execute our collective visions and lead our group to prosperity.

I realized that if I wanted to thrive as a leader, I had to be selfless. I had to know that taking care of myself wouldn't diminish that selflessness but would help me increase the stamina of my selflessness. My confidence lies between knowledge of myself and knowledge of my purpose. Once I tapped into that confidence, it was much easier for me to be comfortable with selling my ideas in order to get people to back my ideas. I became ready to gain a significant following. I'd gathered the necessary tools I needed to help me sustain an accurate understanding of who I am at every stage, so I could consciously affect the power of my influence that has revealed its weight to me repeatedly. In order for me to thrive as a great leader, I had to understand my potential impact at each level: influence, power, and responsibility.

The impact of my influence is directly correlated with the number of people I can reach and convert to my beliefs.

The impact of my power is directly correlated to my decision-making abilities, regardless of the decision I make. If I'm in a position where I can make the decision, then I have power. Understanding my power in this way has allowed me to decide what's best for me and my team.

The impact of my responsibility is a different beast though. It's a beast with many different personalities in the form of allegiances, each appearing whenever called upon. For example, if you're a CEO, your responsibility to your shareholders is just as important as your responsibility to your customers and employees. The ability to understand that you can't have one without the other and to balance the two to make the best decisions is a skill reserved for the best leaders. The responsibilities required of you are very different for each. A combination of experience and a natural talent for reading situations separates the great leaders from the not-so-great leaders. For me to thrive in my purpose, I had to figure out what my responsibilities were. As I went through all my roles—writer, entrepreneur, son, brother, friend, etc.— there were common characteristics that I felt I was responsible for. Being smart, honest, and purposeful led the charge.

The legends I'm named after were all leaders, each with their own individual style, who rallied millions of people. Stevie Wonder was able to rise above a lifelong disability to become one of the greatest artists of all time, using his voice to promote love and uplift not only Black people but people around the world from every ethnicity. He inspired a generation to rise above the misfortune life threw at them to find the gifts that it offers. After gaining fame from those gifts, he used his voice not only to help heal through his music but also to advocate for a number of social justice issues, including helping to advance Black civil rights awareness by leading the effort to make Martin Luther King Jr.'s birthday a national holiday. The impact has and continues to positively impact millions every year as the country not only remembers but gets together to complete thousands of acts of service in his honor. This speaks to MLK's leadership. Years after his assassination, his views on love, service, and humanity continue to outlast the hate that caused his assassination. This hate caused Malcolm X's leadership style to be more militant and extreme than Martin's. I've recently been thinking a lot about what kind of leader I want to be, a side effect of this healing journey I embarked on. I want to try and be as intentional about it as possible and approach it as more of an art than a science. With so many different influences embedded in my name, I've tried searching for a balance that represents my actual thoughts rather than trying to imitate these legends I'm named after. If leaders are confused about what they represent, then how will they gain any followers? What I've found is that extreme humanism is the leadership style that best represents my vision for the world. And if I'm going to thrive in this world, that's how I want to do it.

VISION FIRST

It wasn't until the vision I held of myself became negative that I realized the power of each end of the vision spectrum, how it could either advance or destroy me. The way I viewed myself was directly correlated to my actions. Focusing on who I wanted to be instead of who I thought I was helped me release the negative images I held of myself. It helped me power through fear. I remember I used to get frustrated when people couldn't see my vision as I'd laid it out. It took some time for me to see that the vision I had for my life was mine and mine alone. No one else could see it, so it was my responsibility to learn how to properly communicate it to myself and others. That's why it was so important for me to believe in myself even if I couldn't feel it. Before my grief and depression took over me, I never had a problem with advocating for myself. What this healing journey has taught me was the importance of advocating to myself for myself. It became so easy for society, family, friends, and everyone in between to project their reality on me that I began believing that the visions I had for myself were out of reach. It seemed like no one else could see it. Every day, I had to consciously reaffirm my belief in myself and my visions. Reflecting on my experiences helped me remember the times when I believed in myself enough to chase my vision and make it a reality. My hindsight view showed me the shift that occurred every time. I could see how I expanded others' perception of what's possible. I saw this firsthand with my family, with my dad pushing himself to move up in rank at work, my brother starting his own business, and my mom rebranding herself after retirement. Not to take credit for anyone's accomplishment, but actions become cyclical. It's what gets passed down from generation to generation, yes, but it also gets passed across to permeate existing generations.

Manifestation for me is the process of making my vision a

reality. I never knew there was a word for it until I began to dig deeper into spirituality. I saw that it's nothing more than the energy that feeds action. It's momentum. After putting a name to what had gotten me the success I'd already achieved, I knew that to step into thrive mode I had to put a process to it as well. The first step in my manifestation process became acknowledging that my vision has merit and accepting it as a possible reality for myself, no matter what it is. Whether it was a vision of living a healthier lifestyle or a vision of landing a job, it was all in the details. I recognized just how small a being I was living in an infinite universe. It took me traveling the world to understand just how small I was. When you've been regulated to a four-block radius for most of your life, your perspective can become distorted.

Now, during my meditations, I try to focus on manifesting how I'd like my day, week, month, or year to go. I imagine myself at the center of the universe with the power to shift energy in any direction I want, energy that often comes to me through streaks of color until the color shapes itself into a symbol. At this point, I can see nothing else but this symbol that represents the very thing I'm attempting to manifest in my life. Then there's nothing but me, this thing, space, and opportunity. Manifestating is a small act, but it has a huge impact. The significance of this resides in helping me believe this outcome that I envision is possible because it puts me in tune with the feelings and emotions its reality invokes. I feel the energy of a successful presentation before I present. I feel the energy of writing a successful chapter before it is written. I feel the energy of being a successful entrepreneur, and I'll continue to pursue the reality of that feeling. Next, I will launch the vision I have into the universe as if I'm writing it into law. It's intentional. I'm manually reprogramming my mind to release doubt and increase hope. It helps me gain clarity on my vision so that I can figure out my next action steps because action is always the most crucial step in manifesting my visions. I use the word *vision* instead of *dream* because *dream* to me carries the energy of something that is out of reach; the word *vision* carries the energy of something real that brings clarity. You may have heard the phrase, "Faith without works is dead." Whether you're religious, spiritual, both, or neither, action is always the key. Not to romanticize action as this big grand gesture that you need to do, it's just one step forward followed by another and another. It's not always as dramatic as a leap but it always feels like magic when complete.

Having a growth mindset was always vital for me on my journey, especially due to my lack of resources. It's allowed me to get comfortable with starting at the bottom of whatever endeavor I decided to pursue. Before I knew it, I would find myself with new visions as I began living out the old ones. My growth mindset is what helped me stick with practicing meditation.

The more self-aware I became, the clearer I became on what my internal barriers were. Meditation helped illuminate them, creating an internal light that traveled through my mind to its source, leading to more intentional and detailed meditations. Once I started to feel a physical connection with the universe and its infinite energy, I saw possibilities in what seemed like a different dimension that I could tap into whenever I wanted, with the power to direct the reality of my physical one. While in this tranquil trance part of my process of manifestation, I was asking the universe to remove any external barriers that I wasn't aware of. I exerted an energy that allowed me to release the weight of worry from my shoulders and helped me to accept the things I couldn't control, which became a huge stress reliever. I began to thrive in a whole new way once I found peace in connecting with Allah, the universe, and myself. If the three of us couldn't make something happen, then I knew it wasn't meant to be. I just had to make sure I did my part and, when I didn't, I could tell because the darkness between my reality and my vision was too vast, and I couldn't comprehend how to narrow the gap. I experienced this most when I meditated on my grand purpose and went beyond just manifesting my day, week, month, or year.

When I thought about my life's purpose of helping to improve human conditions, the darkness and difficulty I had connecting to its energy made me realize how far I'd strayed from this purpose. I knew that I had to do my part to get back to my natural disposition. This process of meditation and manifestation was helping me do that, but I had to maintain that growth mindset. It was a different experience than prayer but being connected to Allah helped amplify the intensity of the feelings of faith and hope it produced. The spiritual practice of meditating was new to me. I'd always been one to chase my vision but never in this way. Never with so much clarity and direction. I'm by no means an expert on meditation and spirituality, but it's helped me become an expert on me.

At some point, I began to associate fear with an enemy. The best way to deal with an enemy is to confront them head-on and cut off their head. Meditation helped me confront my fears. I envisioned it and then went on offense and strategically began to attack it. Now I scream, "Fuck my enemies!" and it makes me feel like no one can fuck with me anymore. This was how gaining mastery over myself started to make me feel after I began winning my battles with fear. I started to see every possible angle, and I wasn't fazed by it. I could see the whole board. I wasn't afraid to picture the worst outcome in different situations, strengthening my confidence in my ability to recover and defeating fear with a better understanding of life. Death became the only thing I could see that had the ability to stop me. There's no manipulation or strategy that can occur to reverse it. The finality of death used to scare me, but it doesn't anymore because I'm more aware than ever that everyone will die. It's the price we pay for life. Meditation helped me realize that I could have heaven here on earth. Control over myself started feeling much better than the frustrating tug-of-war of trying to control people and things I couldn't change.

Now, I'm clapping for myself! I deserve to celebrate me. Everything is connected and celebrating myself, especially for my small wins, started a chain reaction within me. I had to learn to take the time to celebrate my small victories at every step and remind myself of the power of my manifestations. During my healing journey, specifically my year of stillness, celebrating my small wins became a vital part of my process. Something as simple as rewarding myself with a congratulatory bottle of wine or eating my favorite meal helped me normalize the feeling of accomplishment again. Whether it was the feeling of a breakthrough from a past trauma or calling a friend to strengthen a relationship, the acknowledgment created patience for growth. Once I began to take stock, I found myself winning a lot of small battles from cracking a piece of code on the app I was developing to getting a meeting with someone I admired who could offer advice on how I should navigate. They helped cushion the blow of disappointment, rejection, or any other negative experiences. These battles started holding less emotional weight because I was filling my emotional capacity with positivity. The small wins compounded, and I began enjoying my journey again, without putting too much stress on getting a "big" win. Although, I've yet to stop trying.

Perseverance is important for anyone with a vision because the amount of negative experiences in pursuit of it will be plentiful. The resilience I've built has helped me to balance the emotional impact of negativity and keep my confidence conscious which only reinforced my belief that I could accomplish anything I set my mind to, especially after reflecting on all the small wins I'd failed to properly celebrate throughout my journey thus far. I had to condition myself to believe that I am not my losses. Even when the physical and mental space I was in felt like the sum of them. We get to choose what conditioning to internalize. My new belief system helped me get better at accepting and internalizing praise from others instead of fixating on the negative. I realized that I don't have to have a grandiose win to feel accomplished. The pressure of success had me so focused on an end goal that I lost sight of how much I'd accomplished along the way. I needed time and a lot of reflection to understand this.

My time of reflection, mixed with the process of practicing mindful meditation, is how I began to understand; I was forced to after feeling burned out, unfulfilled, and stuck. Honestly, with everything I had been through and the current state of the world, just getting up and facing the day felt like a courageous act that deserved a round of applause. I had to become mindful of that. Simply doing what I said I was going to do deserved celebration as well. Reading the stories of others helped me recognize that we all face obstacles. I've found that the best things in life are the ones that must be earned, and the downside to pursuing a vision is that any goal I create will come with its own set of obstacles and my personal life will throw in many of its own, whether it's making time to go to the gym when I say I will or starting a new project I've been thinking about. At the very least, I deserved acknowledgment of a job well done. I convinced myself that I deserve to give myself "Grammy Winner Energy." The only difference between my accomplishment and winning a Grammy is the number of people who are clapping and celebrating me. However, even if no one else is clapping, I'm making sure I'm at least clapping for myself. I've decided to thrive in the performance of my many masterpieces and give myself a standing ovation whenever I feel like it. I know now that I'm the only validation I need for my actions to be worthy. Anyone else is just a bonus and I'm at peace with that. I'm seeking to be the best version of me, I'm setting good intentions, and I'm clapping for myself after every hurdle jumped. It's scary sometimes to think about how my vision will continue to grow, but I'm confident in my management of it, knowing that the combination of all my small wins is the recipe for the big ones and that everything is connected and matters. I recognize that my vision of a fruitful, healed life for myself and my community is my strength. I'll no longer suppress it; I'll come alive in it! Who knows, I might just win that Grammy if that's where my journey takes me!

On my journey, I had to figure out a way to beat the system that was designed for me to fail because failure wasn't an option. I can't fail. There's way too much at stake. The more I thought about it, the more I realized that the best way to beat the system is to be happy and to continue the fight for my rights from a place of strength. That's how you thrive. If I wanted to get to the next level, I had to stop playing defense. It was up to me to figure out how to make myself happy. I had to take the time to figure out what that looked like for me beyond safety, security, and survival, which should be bare minimum. I had to drown out all the noise so that I could hear myself, and I always ended up at service to my people. I felt like I had experienced enough of the world to be able to have opinions that I not only respected but loved. Meditation helped me start to really feel that love. It felt like GLORY. I thought I was in a losing stage of my life after losing so much, but my faith in God became strong enough for me to believe that all those setbacks were just setting me up for a life of purpose. I could see the unseen, and they were the signs I needed and asked for. I believed that Allah was preparing me to become the best version of me. It was the only logical explanation after all that I'd sacrificed to make my visions from him come true. I started to feel like this was all part of his test and I wanted to pass. I am more confident in my abilities than ever and I feel ready for everything he showed me I could be. I feel ready to lead on my own with or without the backing of an institution. The only validation I need is myself and that's how I'll thrive.

FORWARD

I wrote this book because I want every Black male to see me and know that anything is possible. All the ups and downs, mountains you'll have to climb, depression, anxiety, and fear, it's all there for a reason. Push through them and never give up. Switch up your pace when the journey gets tough if you need to. Take your time to figure out how to get yourself to the next level, even if you have to go at a snail's pace for a while. Do one small thing every day that works toward your goal. Most importantly, I want everyone who reads this to start or expand on their personal journeys to unconditional self-love. Love yourself today. Unconditional love is the best gift I've ever given myself and it's the gift that keeps on giving. I know I can't meet everybody in the world. Life's just not set up that way, no matter how many people know me or give me a "like" on social media. What I can do is make sure that I make a conscious effort to show love to everyone I cross paths with. Who doesn't want love?

I believe in pushing people by empowering them. My hope is that by telling my story I can empower someone else to tell theirs because they're all important. We're all important and our stories deserve to be told, especially Black stories. The amount of adversity that we've overcome and continue to overcome should be documented and written into history. Realizing that we don't need permission is the single best thing that can happen to a Black person. More and more of us are waking up to this fact and breaking down barriers in all fields. It's a beautiful thing to witness.

I still struggle though. Since I'm being honest, I'm nowhere near where I want to be in my life. This book, for me, is just as important now as it would be if I did accomplish all my goals. I got the courage to write this book by recognizing that I'm already a huge success, even if I'm the only one who sees it. I was and am enough. Unconditional love means loving myself even when my goals seem too distant. We need more celebration of the journey while we're on it. I've learned to embrace the struggle by accepting it as a necessity of existing, I began to become grateful for it. Having problems is a privilege. It means you're alive!

Unfortunately, we can't hide from the chaos of the world

around us. Life is inherently chaotic, and I had to learn how to be calm in the face of it. My self-awareness is what led me to realize how my actions in any given moment are the only thing I can control. Even if things don't work out the way I want them to. I've chosen to be loudly positive because I believe in the power of positive expression to drive civilization into a more just world. Just figuring out how to not let my setbacks define me has allowed me to be more positive. I realized my courage stemmed from the attempt, not the success. If it was easy, it wouldn't be rare. For me, if it's not rare, it's not worth it. We're all rare when we're being ourselves. That's why going forward, I no longer expect people who never attempted anything like what I'm attempting to empathize with my struggle. I know they won't get it and that's OK. They weren't meant to. This is the mindset I needed to cultivate to write this book. I needed to be confident in my attempt. In my mind, it stayed an attempt for the duration of the process until it really started to come together. This is for the people who can find themselves in any part of my story so that they know they're not alone.

Stepping into the thriving season of my life means intentionally stepping out of the shadows and unapologetically taking up space. I'm consciously embracing abundance. Healing myself has given me the wisdom to know that there's always going to be enough for me because my existence has purpose. There's enough love, money, and happiness out there for me to grasp so that I have no reason to be in competition with anyone else. For a long time, I was under the misconception that winning meant beating someone else. My new mindset on winning is being authentically me in all my pursuits and loving myself unconditionally along the way. I'm no longer tying my worth to a specific outcome or my progress toward a goal in comparison to someone else with a similar goal. My moves will now be based on this premise of abundance and not the fear of missing out. That mindset often led me to view others as opponents rather than allies. It's, to me, what can sometimes plague the Black community. We've been conditioned to believe that there is a limited amount of resources available to us, a narrative that has constantly been fed to us through propaganda and followed up with policy creation by our oppressors. It is up to us to reject the notion of scarcity, not the reality of it, but the idea that there's not enough for all of us to be able to attain security and peace. We don't need to take from each other and we don't need to fear giving some of what we have to others. The abundant mindset is one that knows that there will always be enough. As Black people we will always be enough. It's evident simply in our survival which deserves celebration as a whole and individually.

I feel beautiful inside. My heart feels pure again, but, this time, it's met with wisdom from experience. I believe in myself enough to know that I can restore my heart and mind from whatever life throws at me and I can fight through whatever it is that pains me so that I can heal and continue to walk in my purpose. That's my right as a human and I'm claiming my power so I can continue to evolve. One of the craziest things for me to fathom is that after all the things I've been through already, this is still just the beginning. I feel renewed. I'm not sure where I'm going next, but wherever it is, I'm taking a jet to get there. When it's all said and done, I want my legacy to be one reflective of a life spent in the entrenchment of self-love.

FULL CIRCLE

Post-traumatic stress disorder (PTSD) was something I heard people talk about, but never really understood. I never associated myself with having PTSD. To me, it was usually something reserved for soldiers coming out of war zones. But I grew up in Harlem in the '90s during the wild era of the war on drugs; I did come out of a war zone, a war whose sole purpose was to kill and oppress me and anyone that looked like me. This war was created and funded by my own government. At least in actual wartime, you know who your enemy is. As a Black man, I not only dealt with the physical destruction of war, but the psychological destruction became just as deadly. One day I was watching television, and someone explained the symptoms of PTSD. I immediately identified with what they were describing. I did a little more research, and I realized that I had been suffering from PTSD. I never got to the point of being diagnosed. I had stopped going to therapy once my insurance lapsed, but I was aware enough to recognize that I'd been repeatedly reliving all the traumatic events of my life. Placing myself inside the same feelings and experiencing the pain again every time reopened the wound and sometimes created new ones.

The nights of my cousins' deaths had played on a loop in my mind. Part of my healing dealt with trying to gradually decrease the frequency of this happening. It was in the space between each occurrence where I had to learn how to remember those nights without reliving the pain and emotions they invoked. This process took a lot of time and effort. I had to first learn how to be kind enough to myself to allow it. I could no longer torture myself. I had to believe that I deserved compassion. This may seem odd, but when growing up in a war zone, kindness and compassion were usually the last thing you were offered. This caused a domino effect because I started to apply this process to all the past traumatic events of my life that still haunted me. "Honor the memory without reliving the pain. Be kind to yourself." This became my mantra. My main defense against trauma. I'm done living in the past. The vision I have of my future is relegated to positively impacting as many people as possible. My present actions will forever be dictated by my visions of the future. Life is a dream. Create yours and live inside its bubble. Legendary shit.

ABOUT ATMOSPHERE PRESS

Founded in 2015, Atmosphere Press was built on the principles of Honesty, Transparency, Professionalism, Kindness, and Making Your Book Awesome. As an ethical and author-friendly hybrid press, we stay true to that founding mission today.

If you're a reader, enter our giveaway for a free book here:

SCAN TO ENTER
BOOK GIVEAWAY

If you're a writer, submit your manuscript for consideration here:

SCAN TO SUBMIT
MANUSCRIPT

And always feel free to visit Atmosphere Press and our authors online at atmospherepress.com. See you there soon!

AUTHOR BIO

STEVLAND POLITE is a technologist, business person, and world traveler. He was born and raised in East Harlem, New York, by his loving parents before embarking on a journey across more than twenty countries. He currently serves as a Vice President of Technology at one of the most prestigious investment banks in the world. He loves music, books, and theater. Today, Stevland lives in Central Harlem, New York, and remains adamant about preserving the culture of Black people in his hometown. He's also an advocate for the wellness of Black people across the diaspora.